marionettes

and String Puppets Collector's Reference Guide

marionettes

and String Puppets Collector's Reference Guide

by Daniel E. Hodges

ANTIQUE TRADER BOOKS
A Division of Landmark Specialty Publications
Norfolk, Virginia

To my father, Roy, who told me "it will stop hurting as soon as the pain is gone."

ISBN 0-930625-94-3
Library of Congress Catalog Card Number: 98-71058

Editor: Tony Lillis
Designer: Chris Decker
Copy Editor: Sandra Holcombe
Editorial Assistant: Wendy Chia-Klesch

Printed in the United States of America

To order additional copies of this book, or to obtain a catalog, please contact:

Antique Trader Books
P.O. Box 1050
Dubuque, Iowa 52004
or call 1-800-334-7165

Table of Contents

Foreword

For hundreds of years, children laughed, cried, and learned through the world of string puppetry—what we now call marionettes. It was a form of communication performed from village to village that, along with the balladeers, conveyed messages of news and gossip, along with lessons in manners, religion, kindness, and other virtues. This was a time before the newspapers, magazines, radio, and television. This was a time when much of the population lived widely apart, and the string puppets and marionettes were a connection to each community.

The use of marionettes as a communication tool diminished over the generations, to become a pure form of entertainment that kept the children occupied as the adults found pleasure in the fortune telling, games, and fun provided by the wandering groups of Gypsies who created the first "carnivals." In these later years, marionettes began to co-exist with the art of hand puppetry, and its most famous play, *Punch and Judy.*

As the world changed and grew, puppets and marionettes became less popular, replaced by invention after invention that caught the attention of adult and child alike. The voluminous discovery of so many new things caused the U.S. patent office to close its doors for a few months in the mid-1890s, "as everything has been invented." Upon its re-opening, one of the first items to be patented was a new string method for marionettes.

This first volume of *Marionettes and String Puppets Collector's Reference Guide,* by Daniel E. Hodges, does its job. Its goal is to make the rich research material available for the first time in a readable, workable approach to the subject of string puppets and marionettes. You will find that Hodges' ability to focus on a very specific area of interest allows the collector to be treated to knowledge that may never have been seen.

Collectors in any field who study and learn more about their interests actually obtain more pleasure from the hobby, because with the new knowledge comes appreciation. Even if your interest is only slight or runs very deep, this volume will surely bring new appreciation to your hobby.

Patricia R. Smith
April 1998

Acknowledgments

Thank you to the following people who, through their sharing of knowledge, time, and materials, helped make this book a reality: Steve Alexander, Des Moines, IA; The Reverend and Mrs. Ralph Bagger, Allentown, PA; Pat and William Biskie, Port Byron, IL; Carmen, Gary, and Albee Busk, Carrollton, TX; Temmie Flemming, Salt Lake City, UT; Diane Houk, Independence, MO; Daniel S. Jacoby, Longboat Key, FL; the late Mike Joly, Sterling Heights, MI; Jeff Judson, Flemington, NJ; David Leech, Waymouth, Dorset; Steven Meltzer, Venice, CA; Bruce Pierce, Des Moines, IA; Gary Schneider, Seattle, WA; Mike Tammaro, Stoneham, MA; Mike Weir, North Hollywood, CA; and Linda Williams, Seffner, FL.

Thank you to Steve Alexander, Alexander's Photo Center, for sharing his photographic expertise, advice, and guidance. Thank you to Pat and William Biskie for allowing me to photograph their Collection of Tony Sarg marionettes. Thank you to David Leech whose publication *Yours Puppetually* was the primary source of information for the Pelham Puppets section.

A tremendous thank you to Carmen and Gary Busk for their overwhelming hospitality and generosity in sharing their home, knowledge, time, and marionette collection with me. Their assistance and input contributed immensely in the completion of this book.

A special thank you to my wife, Mindy, who not only suffered through the final stages of my completing this book, but did so while also enduring a fractured knee and numerous surgeries. Thank you all!

Daniel E. Hodges

Introduction

How do we become collectors? Does it start in the crib when adults bombard us with a variety of items to touch, hold, tickle, and taste? Does our pleasure in being surrounded by lots of toys lead to our desire to acquire? If having more than one is fun, then having eight is great! We graduate from childhood collections (like bottle caps and shiny stones), which cost us nothing, to accumulating special interest items which can cost us a lot.

When I was growing up, marionettes were all the rage. Tony Sarg was the name that everybody knew. Stringpullers ruled the roost, and anywhere they appeared, they were bound to draw a crowd and sell out. The novelty of seeing miniature players on a miniature stage mesmerized audiences, but visits by touring companies were few and far between. Manufacturers realized they could fill the gap by selling a cast of toy-sized characters to potential puppeteers. Kids could put on shows at home, and adults could untangle the strings. All this was in the innocent pre-TV days, before children were a target market to be manipulated by merchandising and hype.

Daniel Hodges has put together a useful guide for collectors covering the history, design, and manufacture of commercial marionettes with a list of present-day sources for collectors. Reading about the companies was a nostalgic trip for me. I remember the Playfellow marionettes of Helen Haiman Joseph, which came in both kit and completed form. F.A.O. Schwartz offered an undressed, carved, wooden figure which could be painted and dressed by the puppeteer. The Swiss import was so well-jointed it could assume many graceful poses even without strings. It is one of my favorite things, and I still have it today, undressed and unstrung. Most marionettes were about the same scale, so they could work together easily. The slight sheen on their painted faces gave them a "professional" look.

I learned of a company called the Hamburg Marionette Guild (Hamburg, NY) from touring professionals Mabel and Cedric Head, of the Kingsland Marionettes. The Guild's first figures were limited to a boy, a girl, and an American Indian. The heads might have been plaster of Paris, for they were very smooth and very heavy. The modeling and painting were masterful. Built on a professional 24-inch scale, the arms and legs were wooden dowels with double screw-eye joints. The felt hands were weighted and the feet were solid lead. The asking price was more than I could afford, but I managed to wheedle the Indian against some future gift occasion. Alas, he turned out to be too tall, too gangly, and too noisy to walk and work on-stage. The buckskin brave retired backstage, and the Guild went out of the manufacturing business without creating anything new.

That memory pointed out the differences between "then" and "now." A child sees the marionette as an action figure to be used in a show which adults will sit down to watch. An adult sees the marionettes as toys evoking the spirit of childhood, to be preserved, encased, enshrined, and admired, but definitely on inactive status. And we have all been educated by the Barbie collectors that the value goes up if the object has never been out of the box.

I was glad that Mr. Hodges included Homemade in his listings, for many of us started with the help of Edith Flack Ackley's book, *Marionettes: Easy to Make, Fun to Use!* There were patterns for the stuffed muslin marionettes tucked in a flap in the back of her book. Sewing and stuffing were in the skill range of an eight year old. *McCall's* magazine also published a playscript of hers, with patterns and directions for sewing the characters and staging a play. The first marionette I ever made was from a Flack Ackley pattern.

As "grown-ups" we now have the patience to untangle the strings without resorting to tantrums. That is a change for the better. But there are some things about your collection that will never change. The dreams of a child are still there right behind the eyes.

George Latshaw
April 1998

How to use this book

This book is intended to serve as a point of reference, a guide to aid in identifying marionette characters and their makers. It will introduce you to the various makers, and describe what characters were made, who made them, when they were made, what they were made of, and provide information on how to date certain marionette characters.

The values listed in this book are to serve as a reference, and are based on marionettes in near-mint condition. These values are not scripture and should be used as a guide only. Values of certain marionettes on either coast and near metropolitan areas may be higher. Sought-after characters such as those from *The Howdy Doody Show* and Disney characters will also bring higher values.

How values were determined

The values are based on prices of marionettes and string puppets sold, purchased, and advertised over a period of five-plus years. Classified ads, auctions, antique shows, flea markets, and antique and collectible stores have been included as sources for those prices. Geographically, prices were obtained from all over the United States. Prices from Canada, Germany, and England have been considered, also. After having established values, those said values were then reviewed by other collectors/dealers to assure that they are reasonable.

A brief history

String puppets have existed for hundreds of years and have been a part of many cultures. Legend suggests that string puppets existed in the Orient as early as 1000 B.C. Remnants of puppet-like figures made out of clay, leather, terra-cotta, and other materials found in archaeological sites of ancient Greece, Persia, and the Far East, could be precursors of string puppets now known as marionettes.

The term "marionette" was first associated with string puppets in sixteenth-century Europe. The origin of the word may be traceable to the Virgin Mary, often the principal character of puppet plays during the 1500s, either as a diminutive of "Maria," or in its literal translation "little Marys," from the French reference to the Virgin.

The early European marionette, known as "A La Planchette," consisted of a string, secured to a post at one end, passing through the body of a jointed puppet or group of puppets. Manipulation of the free end of string, which was often tied to the leg of a minstrel, caused movement and action thereby bringing the puppet(s) to life. By having the string tied to his leg, the minstrel freed up his arms allowing him to play musical instruments to provide music for his puppet show. These marionettes are believed to have originated in Italy where they were called "fantoccini."

Example of "A La Planchette" in detail of early nineteenth-century painting. Giraudon/Art Resource, NY. Develly, Jean Charles, Festival of Saint-Cloud. 1820. Gouache, .315 x .42m. Musee de l'Ile de France, Sceaux, France.

Early puppet shows consisted of roaming minstrels providing impromptu road-side shows for the villagers throughout Europe. As the popularity of these shows grew, their format and presentations became more formal. Theaters were established, and complete plays were performed by the marionettes. Many plays were specifically written for marionettes. In 1573, the first permanent Italian marionette theater was established in London. A number of these puppet theaters were quite elaborate, having a complete complement of props, lighting, scenery, and wardrobes. It was not unusual for the larger theaters to boast of several hundred marionettes in their collection.

During the late 1700s, the composer Joseph Haydn was commissioned to write several operettas for marionettes—and a number of Rossini's operas were adapted to, and performed by, marionettes. Ballets were also produced, with the marionette characters even costumed in tights.

As the skills and craft of the marionette artists were refined, the actions and capabilities of their marionette characters became nearly limitless. Their string puppets could smoke, drink, fire

Example of early marionette in nineteenth-century lithograph. Giraudon/ Art Resource, NY. Vernet, Carle. (after). "The Cries of Paris" No.25: The Merchant of Gingerbread. Color lithograph by Francois Seaphin Delpech (1778-1825). Musee de la Ville de Paris, Musee Carnavalet, Paris, France.

weapons, and be transformed from one object to another, all before the disbelieving eyes of the audience.

Another type of marionette which saw brief use during the 1880s was the "pedal puppet." These marionettes were used in formal theatrical productions. Pedal Puppets were mounted on bases, and movement about the stage was accomplished by shuttling the base below stage level on a series of grooves or tracks. Each marionette character's movement and expressions were controlled by a series of strings running through the puppet connecting to pedals or levers, and manipulated by individuals below the stage. A separate person supplied the vocalizations of the puppet.

Until the late nineteenth century, marionettes were not readily available to the public. In the late 1800s, marionette toys were available in very limited numbers. These marionettes were made by hand, and were primarily made and sold in the same town or geographical area.

It was not until the 1920s that the first commercially made marionette toys were available in the United States. These marionettes were designed by Tony Sarg and sold through New York's B Altman Company. For an advertised price of $4.95, one received two marionette characters and a pressed board stage with curtain and scenery.

Some half dozen companies were commercially producing marionette toys during the 1930s. The increased number of marionette makers reflected the rising public interest in marionettes and puppetry. This increased interest may have been due in part to the numerous books and articles written on puppetry during that time, the abundance of traveling marionette productions throughout the country, or the puppetry programs in the Recreation and Theatre Projects of the Works Progress Administration (W.P.A.).

Interest in marionettes was further fueled during the 1940s and 1950s by the growing popularity of television, and the use of puppets in early children's television programming. This led to shows like *The Small Fry Club*, Disney's *The Mouseketeer Club,* and possibly the most popular show of all, *The Howdy Doody Show*. With its main character a marionette himself, *The Howdy Doody Show* was the catalyst for the skyrocketing marionette frenzy of the fifties. Marionettes were so popular at that time that some companies were advertising hand puppets as "stringless marionettes."

Through the 1950s and 1960s, there were more than two dozen companies making marionettes. As the decade of the 1970s began, the number of companies which made marionettes had dropped to a dozen or less. Many of the marionettes made during the 1970s and 1980s leaned more toward toys or novelties instead of functioning puppets. Three of the exceptions were marionettes and string puppets made by Bob Baker, Pelham Puppets, and Hazelle's. Hazelle's stopped production in the early 1980s. The year 1993 marked the end of the high volume commercial production of marionettes when the Pelham Puppets company closed its doors.

Example of nineteenth-century marionette theater. Victoria & Albert Museum, London/Art Resource, NY. Venetian Marionette Theater. Victoria & Albert Museum, London, Great Britain.

Example of early marionette in 1892 publication. Giraudon/Art Resource, NY. Meyer, Henri. "New Year's in Paris" (The Small Merchants on the Boulevard), Title page to Le Petit Journal, illustrated supplement, 2 January 1892. Private Collection, France.

Collecting marionettes

Are they dolls or toys? Collecting marionettes and string puppets often crosses over into other areas of collecting. It is not unusual to find one or more marionettes included in doll collections. Nor is it out of place for a toy collection to include a marionette or two. Numerous movie, cartoon, and real life characters have been rendered in marionette form such as Dagwood and Blondie Bumstead, Popeye and Olive Oyl, and even pop singers Donny and Marie Osmond.

Collecting Disneyana is an area which frequently intersects with collecting marionettes and string puppets. Disney has had hundreds of licensing arrangements with different companies to produce various Disney products. Dozens of Disney characters have been produced in marionette form, including Mickey and Minnie Mouse, Donald Duck, and the complete cast of characters from Disney's classic animated movie, *Snow White*. Tony Sarg/Madame Alexander, Pelham Puppets, and Peter Puppet Playthings are just a few of the companies that have produced Disney character marionettes.

The Howdy Doody Show has created its own specialty area of collecting, and it, too, crosses over into collecting marionettes. Howdy, his cousin Heidi, Mr. Bluster, Clarabelle, Flubadub, and Princess SummerFall-WinterSpring have all been produced as marionettes. Peter Puppet Playthings was a licensed company for producing *Howdy Doody Show* marionette characters.

Even collecting ephemera can overlap into marionette collecting. Throughout the years a number of different companies have produced paper or cardboard marionettes. The first company may have been the Raphael Tuck and Son Company, which produced a series of paper marionette characters during the early 1900s. Tony Sarg designed a collection of three-dimensional, cardboard marionettes which were available during the early 1940s.

Where does one find marionettes? First, check out your parents' attic or their store room. If you are fortunate, you may find the marionette(s) from your childhood tucked away in a box there. If you are not fortunate, you may learn that, after storing your stuff for 17 years, your folks decided to sell your stuff at their garage sale a month ago. Now you need to begin your search for marionettes elsewhere.

Flea markets are great places to find and buy marionettes. While browsing, keep an eye open for boxes jumbled with dolls or doll parts. Also, watch for those boxes with strings draped or hanging over the sides, and strings dangling from shelves. Remember, though, not all marionettes you come across will have their strings and controls.

Thrift stores such as the Salvation Army and Goodwill are another venue to look into. Usually, these stores will have their merchandise grouped, with toys in one section and dolls in another. Many of these stores have an antiques and collectibles section, too. Be sure to check out all of these areas in the store before you leave.

Auctions are a terrific and fun place to find marionettes. You will increase your odds of finding auctions with marionettes included in the sale if it is a specialty auction, such as a doll or toy auction. That's not to say that you may not come across some great marionette finds at antique, general, or estate auctions.

Check with the auction houses to learn when their sales will be, and if there are going to be any marionettes included. Calling ahead of time can save hours of travel. When calling, ask specifically if any marionettes or string puppets will be included. If the person you are talking to doesn't know what a marionette is (it does happen sometimes), try jogging their memory with Howdy Doody, or the famous goatherd marionette scene in the movie *The Sound of Music*. If both of these fail, ask if there is someone else to talk with or call back later, but be polite. Many auction houses will give you accurate descriptions, though you may need to prompt them in describing the controls, the strings, and if the marionette is plastic, composition, or something else. Some auction houses may offer to send or e-mail you a photograph of the marionette(s).

A word of caution on getting caught up in the fury and the frenzy of bidding at an auction. Set your limits (what is the absolute highest amount you can pay for a given marionette) and stick with them. If you do go over your high bid because you just had to have it, you can console yourself and rationalize your purchase to your spouse with the fact that someone else was willing to pay the amount of the bid prior to yours.

If the auction house is a considerable distance from where you live, and traveling to it is not feasible, inquire if the auction house allows absentee or phone bids. Absentee bidding is when you leave your high bid for the specified items with the auction house prior to the auction. The auction house will then execute your bid for you during the auction. If the bid on an item does not exceed your high bid, you've just purchased a new marionette. Have the auction house FULLY explain their rules and requirements for absentee bidding. Yes, absentee bidding can be a leap of faith for you (trusting the auction house is honest), but it works both ways, too—the auction house is trusting that you will pay what you bid.

Antique shows are nice places to look for marionettes. While browsing the booths at the show, watch for the same things as at the flea-markets. Don't forget to check under the display tables, too. Whether you are at an antique show or flea market, if a dealer has a few dolls or toys for sale in their booth, ask if they have any marionettes or string puppets. You may be pleasantly surprised that they have one or two, they just haven't set them out for display.

Scour the classified ads and sale bills of antique, collectibles, doll, and toy publications. Look for auction ads. Watch for upcoming antique, doll, and toy shows. Learn to look for keywords in the ads: marionettes, string puppets, theaters, etc.

The Internet is an almost boundless place to find marionettes and string puppets. By using the various search engines available, one is able to literally search worldwide. A search engine is a computer program which will search through the various web sites on the Internet for specified keywords, phrases, subjects, and ideas. Because each of the search engines uses different criteria to base its searches, the results will also be different. As an example, using search engine ABC searching on the keywords "Tony Sarg marionettes" could identify eight web sites that have the keywords in them. While using the search engine XYZ, searching on the same keywords could identify only three web sites that contain those same keywords. Because the Internet is dynamic and constantly changing, doing the exact same searches the next day using the same search engines could identify additional sites not listed the day before.

There are a number of web sites on the Internet that have online auctions. Several of these sites have a doll sub-category for marionettes. An online auction functions much the same way a traditional auction functions. The major differences are online auctions can last from a few days to a couple of weeks, and bidding on an item can be done from all over the world. Some online auction sites provide automatic daily updates on the items on which you have bid. Before participating in an online auction, read and fully understand the rules and procedures for each particular auction web site.

Advantages of using the Internet include: It's always "open" 24 hours a day (yes, you could find a mint Effanbee "Lucifer" in Oregon at 2:30 in the morning); it allows you to travel to the corners of the earth from the comfort of your own home; it provides you with a way to look for a specific item (search on "Effanbee marionette") worldwide; and the information is updated almost constantly. There are a number of puppetry and puppet-related web sites, newsgroups, chatrooms, and bulletin boards on the Internet.

Buying and selling marionettes

When buying or selling marionettes through mail order, classified ads, or over the Internet, it is important to protect yourself. Here are a few suggestions to follow to ensure a good transaction for all parties. Both the buyer and seller need to agree on the method of payment, be it check, money order, COD, or credit card. And, depending on the method of payment, how soon the merchandise will be sent. Will the item be insured when sent? If so, at what amount? Will the buyer have the right to return the item if not satisfied upon delivery? If so, establish how many days are reasonable, who pays the shipping, and other issues for consideration for return of the item. Mode of delivery: Will the item be sent UPS, U.S. Postal Service, or other? All of the above should be mutually agreed on by the seller and buyer to ensure satisfaction of all parties of the transaction.

Know what you are buying. Sounds simple. Try to familiarize and educate yourself with the maker and the characters that you are interested in. Learn who made what characters, and what years those marionettes were produced. Know what the marionette character should look like. Did Peter Puppets Playthings' "Cowboy" marionette have a hat or just a holster and gun? Did Pelham Puppets make a blonde, or a brunette, "Red Riding Hood" character? Did Tony Sarg make a plastic marionette? These are the kinds of questions you should ask yourself when making the decision to purchase a marionette.

Watch out for misidentified marionette characters. *The Howdy Doody Show* has probably contributed to those marionette characters most frequently misidentified. Just because a marionette character has a neckerchief, is wearing a checked shirt, or has a western-style outfit on does NOT automatically indicate that specific marionette character is from *The Howdy Doody Show*. Also, the box a marionette is in is not necessarily the original box for that marionette.

Preserving and displaying marionettes

Care for your marionettes depends on what each individual character is made of. Dusting them can be easily done by using a one- or two-inch unused soft bristled paint brush. Caution should be used when cleaning your marionettes. Mild soap, water, and a soft cloth should be used sparingly on plastic, vinyl, and ceramic body parts. Water should not be used on chalk, plaster, or composition body parts as the moisture will cause the material to break down. Soiled clothing may also be cleaned using a soft cloth or sponge with mild soap and water. Test a small area of the fabric being cleaned to test for color fastness.

Tangled strings can be a bane or a blessing. On occasion, a dealer may lower the price for a marionette if the strings appear to be hopelessly tangled. When your marionette's strings do become tangled (and they will) you can choose one of two popular methods to straighten them. The Sit, Pick, and Curse method can be time consuming and may cause you to wish you collected hand puppets instead. The alternative involves untying the strings from the controls first then untangling them. It is much easier to untangle strings with the controls out of the way. The second method, however, is not recommended for those who have flunked remedial knot tying class. To prevent tangled strings, take an untangled marionette. Hold the controls in one hand. With the other hand, spin the body of the puppet. As the marionette is spinning, take hold of the strings at the midpoint. The strings will wind upon themselves. After several windings, wrap the twisted strings around the controls once or twice.

Displaying your marionettes and string puppets is another topic with as many different opinions as there are collectors. It essentially boils down to personal preference and how much space you have available to display your collection. Some collectors remove the strings and controls to reduce the chance of damaging the marionette, and display the marionette using doll stands. Others display their marionettes in vignettes, creating a stage with scenery and props pertaining to the story from which the marionette characters are from. For example, using the Peter Puppet Playthings box set of Alice in Wonderland, one could have Alice addressing the Mad Hatter and March Hare as they are seated enjoying their tea party, in a scene taken from the animated Disney classic. Wall-mounted hat and coat racks make suitable supports to suspend small or large groupings of marionettes and string puppets. Buy a rack with as many pegs or hooks as marionettes that you wish to display. Before suspending your marionettes for display, check their strings for signs of being brittle or frayed.

Marionette (mar′ē ə net′), n. a puppet manipulated from above by strings attached to its jointed limbs.

—*Webster's Encyclopedic Unabridged Dictionary of the English Language*

The following toy makers, big and small, have contributed significantly to the creation, development, and production of many of the most highly regarded and highly sought marionettes and string puppets. Regardless of size or production capacity, and regardless of whether they remained in business for one year or for decades, these enterprises, and the skilled artisans who worked with them, have provided us with joyful memories inspired by their enduring treasures.

Of course, numerous other firms and individuals have also contributed to the long history of marionettes and string puppets, and there is still much more to be learned. Perhaps a reader of this book—it may even be you—will come forward with new information about a heretofore obscure or unheralded toy maker. Or, you may have the good fortune to discover a previously undocumented example of a puppet maker's colorful animated creations.

In the world of antiques and collectibles, it's said that the quest is often as enjoyable as the discovery. For many collectors, further enjoyment comes from the sharing of knowledge and experiences. That sort of sharing is what this book is all about.

American Crayon Company

The American Crayon Company of Sandusky, Ohio, can trace its lineage to the 1890s, when the Western School Supply Company, the Tiffin Crayon Company, and the Parmetor Crayon Company merged into a single entity.

During the 1930s, in addition to their standard products of school supplies, crayons, and paint, American Crayon began production of educational toys. Their educational toys consisted of games, puzzles, trucks, airplanes, and marionettes. These toys were sold by the American Crayon Company in both finished items, and unfinished, do-it-yourself kits.

Made in the "box shop" (so called because that is where the small wooden boxes to hold the crayons were originally made) in Sandusky, the marionettes had wood block bodies and shaped-wood hands and feet. The heads of the marionettes are chalk, composition, or wood.

Above: Puppinetts Canister: Canister for clown kit; Label reads "designed by Franc Still, Cleveland OH"; 1930s. (Carmen & Gary Busk Collection)

Box cover: Marked "The American Crayon Company, Sandusky OH, New York"; 1930s. (Carmen & Gary Busk Collection)

Detail of box cover depicting other puppets available. (Carmen & Gary Busk Collection)

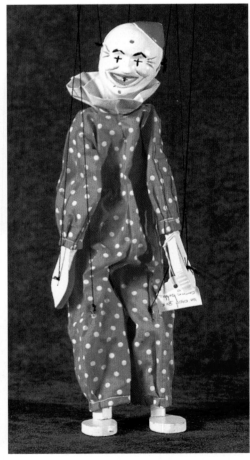

Clown: Plaster head; Wood hands and feet; 1930s; $60-80. (Carmen & Gary Busk Collection)

Badger Cutouts, Inc.

Located in Maspeth, Long Island, New York, during the 1940s, Badger Cutouts, Inc., produced a series of animal marionettes. Their "Pup-Pet" marionette characters include "Quacky" the duck, "Nosey" the hound, "Frisky" the colt, "Kitty," and "Bunny."

Badger's "Pup-Pets" came in 8-1/2-inch by 11-inch envelopes, which contained the cutout colorful paper pieces which, when assembled using tabs and string, created the two-dimensional marionette characters. Manipulation of these paper marionettes was controlled through a paper control.

Bunny: Heavy paper/cardboard construction; 1940s; $25-40. (Carmen & Gary Busk Collection)

Quacky: Heavy paper/cardboard construction; 1940s; $25-40. (Carmen & Gary Busk Collection)

Nosey: Heavy paper/cardboard construction; 1940s; $25-40. (Carmen & Gary Busk Collection)

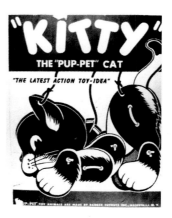

Kitty: Heavy paper/cardboard construction; 1940s; $25-40. (Carmen & Gary Busk Collection)

Bob Baker Marionettes

Bob Baker, a renowned puppeteer in his own right, began making marionettes commercially in the mid-1940s. Early Bob Baker marionettes have composition heads, wood feet, legs and hands, and wood block bodies. Later, marionette characters utilized a rubber tubing for the arms and legs. Depending on the character, Bob Baker marionettes vary from 16 to 22 inches in height.

Some of the different marionette characters available from Bob Baker were: Colored boy and girl, Dutch boy and girl, a sailor, a dog, and Bobo the Clown. Two key elements in identifying these marionettes are the wedge shaped wood feet/shoes and the uniquely shaped flat wood hands.

Bob Baker has been the maker of the numbered limited edition marionettes available at the popular Disney stores since the early 1980s. These special marionettes range from two to more than four feet in height.

The Bob Baker Marionette Theatre, located in Los Angeles, has been long established and highly recognized for the marionette productions staged there. Bob Baker marionettes are still available today.

Pinocchio: Copyright Disney; 18 inches tall; Available through Disney theme parks, and stores; $300-$500. (Carmen & Gary Busk Collection)

Bobo the Clown(s): 1980s; $125-150. (Carmen & Gary Busk Collection)

Ballerina and Suzy: 1950s; $125-150. (Carmen & Gary Busk Collection)

Pinocchio: Copyright Disney; Prototype; $100-125. (Carmen & Gary Busk Collection)

Minnie and Mickey Mouse: Copyright Disney; 1970 reproductions from originals first licensed to and made by Hestwoods in the 1930s; These are numbered limited editions; $350-500. (Carmen & Gary Busk Collection)

Detail from undated advertisement. (Carmen & Gary Busk Collection)

Right: Detail from undated advertisement. (Carmen & Gary Busk Collection)

Pinocchio: Copyright Disney; Disney version; $100-125. (Carmen & Gary Busk Collection)

Claudette's Handmade Marionettes

Very little is known about this marionette maker, which was based in the Kansas City suburb of Mission, Kansas, and located in the Playhouse Studio on 53rd Street. Claudette's marionettes are believed to have been made sometime during the 1950s.

The marionette's painted composition head and arms are the same size used for small baby dolls. The body is made of wood blocks and the shoes/feet are also composition. The controls are made from two wooden dowels and are attached to the marionette with six strings.

Curtis Crafts

Virginia Austin, an accomplished puppeteer and designer, was the creator of the "little clown with the big heart" marionette "Clippo the Clown." During the early 1930s, Virginia Austin was selling Clippo the Clown marionettes independently. The Effanbee Company purchased the rights to Clippo, and employed Virginia Austin to create, design, and demonstrate additional marionette characters for their Clippo line of Effanbee marionettes.

After leaving Effanbee and reacquiring the rights to Clippo, Virginia continued to make Clippo the Clown and a number of new characters through her own company, Curtis Crafts. Curtis Crafts was originally located in Easton, Connecticut. Curtis was Virginia Austin's married name.

One of Curtis Crafts' more popular characters was "Tizzie." Tizzie's creation had been commissioned by Parents Institute, the publishers of *Parents* and *Polly Pigtails* magazines. Tizzie had a wood block body, a composition head with painted features, composition hands and feet. She sported yellow yarn pigtails, and wore a checked shirt and blue shorts. The heel of each of Tizzie's shoes is marked "Curtis Crafts, Made in USA." Tizzie stands approximately 15 inches tall, and is controlled by nine strings.

Virginia Austin, in addition to her talents as a puppeteer, was a gifted sculptress. She made the original version of "Mortimer Snerd" for Edgar Bergen.

Virginia Austin continued to create marionette characters up to the early 1980s.

Clown: Paper label on controls; Playhouse Studio phone Hedrick 0724; 55513 West 53rd Street, Mission, Kansas; Composition head, hands, and feet; 24 inches tall; 1950s; $35-50. (Author's Collection)

Clippo the Clown: Marked "Clippo, V. Austin" on base of neck; 1960s; $75-100. (Carmen & Gary Busk Collection)

Polly Pigtail: Marked "V. Austin, Polly Pigtail" on base of neck; "Curtis Crafts made in USA" on heels of shoes; 1940s; $90-125. (Author's Collection)

Polly Pigtail: Marked "V. Austin, Polly Pigtail" on base of neck; "Curtis Crafts made in USA" on heels of shoes; 1940s; $90-125. (Carmen & Gary Busk Collection)

Elephant: Made with gray velveteen cloth; 1970s; $175-225. (Carmen & Gary Busk Collection)

Tiz 'n Whiz: Undated advertisement. (Carmen & Gary Busk Collection)

Effanbee

During the 1930s, the Fleischaker and Baum Company, better known as "Effanbee," sold the Clippo series of marionettes in addition to the many famous dolls. The headlining character, for which this series was named, was Clippo the Clown. These marionettes were created and designed by the accomplished puppeteer Virginia Austin, who originally made and sold Clippo in the early 1930s. Effanbee obtained the rights to make and sell the Clippo marionettes from Austin, whom they employed to create, develop, and promote their marionette line. Other characters in the line included: Lucifer, Leeza Leah, and Emily Ann.

Effanbee marionettes have wood block bodies, composition heads, hands, and feet, painted features, molded and yarn hair. The marks for these marionettes are usually located on the lower rear base of the puppets' heads. When present, the marks may be as follows: the character's name on the first line, the word "Effanbee" or the letters "FB" on the second line and the name "V. Austin" on the final line. In keeping with the Effanbee tradition, the Clippo series of marionettes also came with the company's "Golden Heart" wrist tag.

Effanbee also sold "Workshop Puppets." These were kits which contained all the materials needed to assemble one or more marionette characters, depending on the kit.

In the late 1930s, Effanbee dropped their marionette line, and Virginia Austin reacquired the rights to Clippo. She continued making Clippo marionettes, and created several new characters through her own company, Curtis Crafts.

Effanbee briefly added marionettes to their product line again as they marketed the Talentoy marionettes in 1948. These puppets were imported and finished by the Talen-Products Company, and distributed through Effanbee.

Top and Top Right: Clippo the Clown: Composition head and hands; 1930s; $85-125. (Author's Collection)

Right: Clippo: Close-up of golden heart tag.

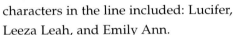

Right: "Clippo" Workshop Puppet: Finished man; 1930s; $125-150. (Carmen & Gary Busk Collection)

Left: "Clippo" sign: Cardboard; 1930s. (Carmen & Gary Busk Collection)

Lucifer: Composition head, hands, and feet. Marked "Lucifer, V. Austin, Effanbee" on back of neck; 1930s; $250-350. (Carmen & Gary Busk Collection)

Lucifer. (Carmen & Gary Busk Collection)

Emily Ann: Composition head, hands, and feet; 1930s; $100-150. (Carmen & Gary Busk Collection)

Workshop Puppets: Box Cover; 1930s. (Author's Collection)

Pet Pup: 1930s; $200-300. (Carmen & Gary Busk Collection)

Right: "Clippo" Workshop Puppets (girl): 1930s; $125-150. (Carmen & Gary Busk Collection)

Gund

Gund, a name synonymous with stuffed animals and teddy bears, was also a purveyor of marionettes. Founded in 1898 by Adolph Gund, the first wares sold by his company included belts, necklaces, novelties, and handmade stuffed toys. Adolph Gund retired in 1925 and sold the company on condition that the Gund name be kept.

During the mid-1960s, Gund made and sold a number of different marionette characters. Gund marionettes were produced in Brooklyn, New York, at Gunderland Park, the world headquarters for Gund. According to Gund Company records, their first marionettes appeared in 1964. Marionettes were a part of the Gund product line until 1968, when they last appeared in company catalogs.

Popular television cartoons and animated movies again provided the source for the marionette characters made by Gund. Walt Disney characters included Mickey Mouse, Donald Duck, Pinocchio, and Jiminy Cricket. Popeye, Olive Oyl, and Brutus were the characters representing King Features cartoons.

Another popular set of Gund marionette characters were those based on the animated character "Koko the Clown," originally created by Max and Dave Fleischer. The "Out of the Inkwell" cartoons, produced by Hal Seeger Productions, re-introduced Koko the Clown through some 100 five-minute television episodes broadcast during the 1960s. In this cartoon series Koko was paired with a girlfriend "Kokette," his dog "Kokonut," and an arch-rival by the name of "Mean Moe."

Gund marionettes are approximately 12 inches in height. The familiar "Gund" cloth tag was sewn into the costume of their marionettes. Their upper bodies

Top: Mickey Mouse: Marked "copyright W.D.P" on back of head; 1960s; $75-100. (Carmen & Gary Busk Collection)

Left: Jiminy Cricket: 1960s; $50-70. (Carmen & Gary Busk Collection)

are of wood block, and the lower bodies consist of stuffed cloth. The heads, hands, and feet are made of molded vinyl. The heads may look familiar to collectors of hand puppets as Gund would use the same head molds for both their hand puppets and their marionettes. The "One Hand Control" controls are plastic, and are an updated version based on the design patented by Raye Copeland in 1953, and used by Peter Puppet Playthings for their marionettes. Peter Puppet advertised the design as the "Unitrol" and made their controls out of cardboard.

Olive Oyl: Soft cloth body; Gund tag; 1960s; $40-60. (Author's Collection)

Pinocchio: 1960s; $75-100. (Carmen & Gary Busk Collection)

television characters

Television, it could be argued, has been the boon and the bane of marionette popularity. From the 1940s through the 1960s, television programming contributed a steady supply of popular characters to be made as marionettes and marketed to the masses. Many of these television shows utilized the magic of puppets and puppetry in the production of their programs. Hand puppets, rod puppets and marionettes were used extensively. Peter Puppet Playthings and Pelham Puppets both made some of the more popular television marionette characters, based on shows like *Howdy Doody*, *The Bob Emery Show*, *The Merry Mailman*, *The Thunderbirds*, and *Archie Andrews*. Both in the United States and Europe, television was a powerful influence on the popularity of marionettes.

Hazelle's, Inc.

Perhaps the most prolific manufacturer of marionettes in the United States was Hazelle's, Incorporated. This Kansas City, Missouri-based company was founded by Hazelle Hedges in the 1930s. During their forty-plus years of business, Hazelle's, Incorporated produced several hundred different marionette characters.

Marionettes made by Hazelle's prior to 1949 have carved wood or molded, lacquered, sawdust, and glue composition heads, distinctively shaped wood hands, wood block body parts, and painted wood feet/shoes. The process to season the composition head took thirty days to complete. Each individual marionette's facial features were then hand painted. Mohair and wool crepe was used for the puppet's hair. These early Hazelle's marionettes are approximately 12 to 14 inches tall, depending on the character.

In 1949, Hazelle's began using a new injection molded plastic process. This new process made use of a hard plastic called Tenite. Marionettes made after the mid-1940s had head, hands, and feet made of injection molded Tenite, while the body parts continued to be made from wood blocks. During the late 1950s and early 1960s, Hazelle's began using vinyl for some of their marionette characters. A complete series of marionettes, the 700 "Beginners" series, had their head, arms, and feet made exclusively of soft touch vinyl.

Hazelle's marionettes may be identified by a three-digit series number, character name, and the year in which it was produced. The series number represented the different features of the marionettes and their various price ranges. An undated salmon-colored catalog from the 1940s lists 22 characters in the new 700 series. The highlighted character in this catalog was number 700, "White Faced Clown." This marionette appears to be an early example of the character later known as number 801, "Teto." Also listed in this catalog are 18 "Deluxe" marionettes comprising Hazelle's 300 series, and two 600 series "Talking" marionettes. The Hazelle's catalog for 1950 details the 400 "Talking" marionettes series, the 900 "Lifelike" series, and the 800 "Popular" marionettes series. From the mid-1950s until the late 1970s, 300 denoted the "Talking" series, 400 denoted the "Deluxe" series, and 800 denoted the "Popular" series. In the early 1960s, 700 became the "Beginners" series.

Over the years, Hazelle's dropped and reused many series numbers and character names, so it becomes necessary to utilize year made, series number, and character name to correctly identify a puppet. For example, in 1956, the character name for the series number 804 was "Tomboy." In 1962, the character name for the same series number was "Voodoo Witch." Another situation occurs when the series num-

Fairy Godmother: Composition head, painted features. (Author's Collection)

Bottom and top detail of 1930s wood hand. (Author's Collection)

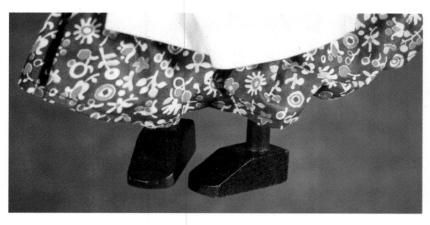

Example of early feet/shoes: 1930s. (Author's Collection)

ber remained the same marionette, but its character name changed. In 1962, the character name for series number 312 was "Pinocchio," but by 1972, the name had changed to "Swiss Boy." One of the first things to look for in identifying Hazelle's marionettes is the controls. Original puppets have the patented vermilion red-colored "airplane" control. Early (1930s through mid-1940s) controls are ink stamped with "Hazelle's" and patent pending or patent numbers. Later controls have the "Hazelle's" paper label affixed to them.

Penny: No. 810; 1962. (Author's Collection)

Left: 1930s "airplane" control: Ink stamped "Hazelle's". (Author's Collection)

The 800 "Popular" series marionette characters were Hazelle's lower-end priced marionettes. These puppets did not have the extra features or the fancy outfits that the more expensive 300 "Special" and 400 "Deluxe" series puppets had. Features of the "Popular" series included hand-painted facial features, head, hands, and feet/shoes, made of Tenite, Mohair, or wool crepe hair, and the patented airplane controls. According to Hazelle's advertisement claims, their all-time best-selling marionette character was from the 800 "Popular" series and was number 801, "Teto the Clown."

The 300 "Special" series marionettes were the middle-range-priced marionettes. These mari-

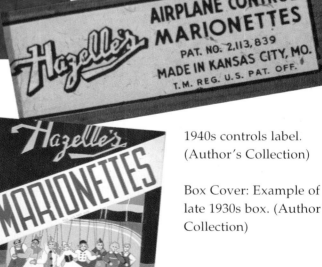

1940s controls label. (Author's Collection)

Box Cover: Example of late 1930s box. (Author's Collection)

onettes had all the features as the 800 series, plus Hazelle's patented "one touch" talking feature. Puppets with this feature had a movable mouth which was controlled through the manipulation of an additional eighth string attached to the controls. The height of these marionettes is 15 to 16 inches.

The 400 "Deluxe" series were Hazelle's high-end priced marionettes. Their features included the same as the lesser priced marionettes, plus more. These puppets are taller, 15 to 17 inches tall, and they have fancier outfits and costumes. Brightly colored silks, satins, and laces were fashioned into glamorous gowns, dresses, suits, and tuxedos for the "Deluxe" characters. These marionettes were Hazelle's show-stoppers.

The 700 "Beginner" series, introduced in the early 1960s, were designed by Hazelle's for use by small children. These marionettes are made from soft touch vinyl. They have the simpler and smaller vermilion red colored T-bar controls. Fewer strings and easier manipulation made these 11- to 14-inch marionettes ideal for developing puppetry skills.

Hazelle's marionettes could be purchased individually or in box sets. Mail order catalog/brochures were included with the marionettes. These listed and pictured other marionette characters and accessories which were available from Hazelle's. Stages, props, kits, and display stands were among the items available. Also included with the puppets were short plays written for the marionette characters.

Box sets included two or more marionette characters (theme or story related), and in addition,

Sample pages of 1940s and 1950s catalogs. (Author's Collection)

had props and scenery, and some sets had lighted stages. One box set, featuring early composition puppets, was the 400 series, "Cinderella." This two box set included "Poor Cinderella," "Rich Cinderella," "Fairy Godmother," and "Prince Charming" (complete with slipper in hand). Other box sets include 403, "The Three Little Pigs;" 404, "The Tower Princess;" 405, "Doris' Broadway Debut;" plus many more.

Hazelle's also sold "hobby kits." These kits contained all the parts necessary to assemble one or more marionette characters. Everything to make "your own" puppet was included in the kit, even the needle and thread.

Hazelle Hedges held patents for a number of marionette features. An early patent, number 2,113,839, granted in 1938, was for her design of the marionette controls and the puppet's construction. These designs provided for a more lifelike manipulation of the marionette.

In 1992, the Puppetry Guild of Greater Kansas City came into the possession of the remaining inventory of the Hazelle's Company. That inventory included finger, hand, and marionette items. Heads, hands, shoes, crepe hair, boxes, wood body parts, controls, clothing, and cardboard stages have been available through the Guild. If you need parts to fix a damaged Hazelle's marionette, contact the Guild.

Sampling of catalog pages from the 1950s, 1960s, and 1970s. (Author's Collection)

Detail of 1956 catalog.
(Author's Collection)

Detail of 1962 catalog.
(Author's Collection)

| 701 | 702 | 703 | 704 | 705 | 706 |
| BOBO CLOWN | MR. RABBIT | MRS. RABBIT | PIRATE | JACK | JILL |

ELLE | 414 DIANE | 415 PRINCESS | 417 MAGIC FAIRY | 418 BALLERINA | 419 FREDDY | 420 MARILY
unette | A modern blond girl | 416 PRINCE

Detail of 1973 catalog.
(Author's Collection)

Mandy: No. 114; Composition head, wool hair; 1930s; $175-225. (Author's Collection)

Mandy: No. 114; controls are ink stamped "Hazelle's Marionettes K.C. MO. - USA PAT PENDING"; 1930s. (Author's Collection)

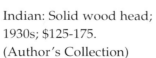

Indian: Painted eyes and mouth. (Author's Collection)

Indian: Feathers of head-dress are missing; note quills still present. (Author's Collection)

Indian: Solid wood head; 1930s; $125-175. (Author's Collection)

Honey Bear: Head, hands, and feet are vinyl; 700 series; Cloth label "created by Hazelle's"; 1960s; $30-50. (Author's Collection)

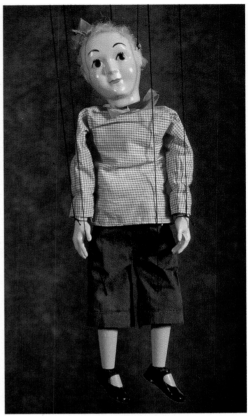

Tom Boy: No. 804; 1953; $30-50. (Author's Collection)

Cinderella: Composition head, painted features; 1930s; $125-175. (Author's Collection)

"Poor" Cinderella. (Author's Collection)

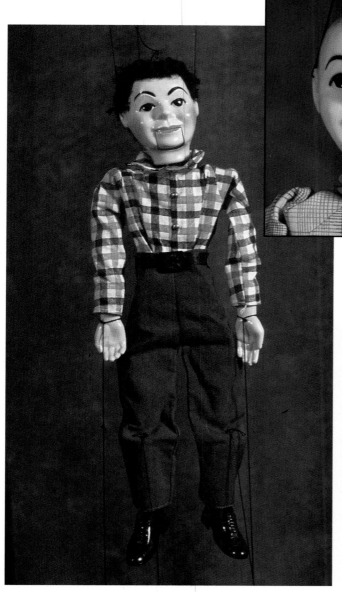

Cowhand: No. 302; mold-
ed hair; $40-60. (Author's
Collection)

Cowhand: No. 302; 1956; $40-60. (Author's Collection)

Alice: No. 306; $40-60. (Author's Collection)

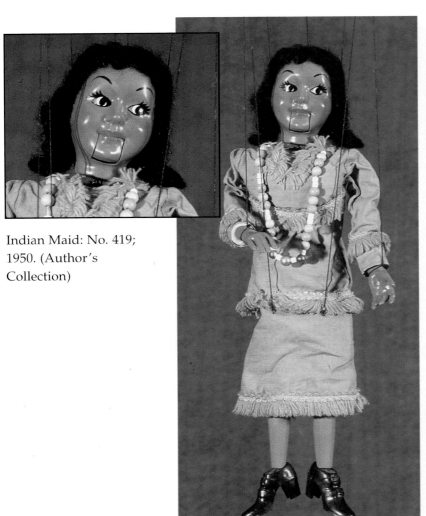

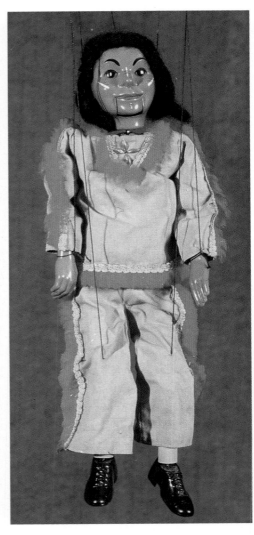

Indian Maid: No. 419; 1950. (Author's Collection)

Indian Maid: No. 419; missing headband and feather; $75-100. (Author's Collection)

Indian Chief: No. 418; missing feather headdress; 1950; $75-100. (Author's Collection)

Right: Hansel: No. 813 in 1962; No. 313 in 1973; $60-80. (Author's Collection)

Far Right: Gretel: No. 814 in 1962; No. 314 in 1973; $60-80. (Author's Collection)

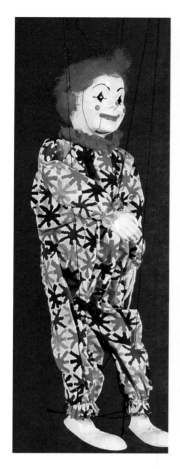

Left: Dwarf/Grandfather: No. 320; In 1962 was called Dwarf; In 1972 was called Grandfather. Tenite head, hands, and feet; $40-60. (Author's Collection)

Suzybell: No 301; 1950s-1970s; $40-60. (Author's Collection)

Above and Right: Fortune Teller: No. 318; Tenite; 1960s-1970s; $40-60. (Author's Collection)

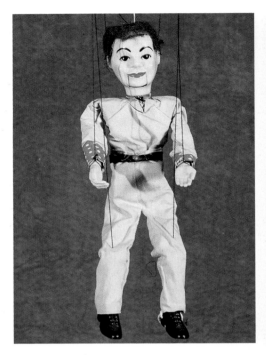

Spaceflyer: No 303; missing neckerchief; 1956; $50-75. (Author's Collection)

Buckeroo Bill: No. 405; Tenite; missing holster with gun and hat; 1950s-1970s; $40-60. (Author's Collection)

Sailor: No. 308; 1973; $40-60. (Author's Collection)

Fairy Godmother: No. 400; Part of Cinderella 2 box set; Composition head, wood hands (note no real feet); 1930s; $150-200. (Author's Collection)

Robin Hood: No. 809 in 1962; No. 319 in 1973; $50-75. (Author's Collection)

TV Tommy: No. 412; 1956; $50-75. (Author's Collection)

Red Riding Hood: No. 818; $40-60. (Author's Collection)

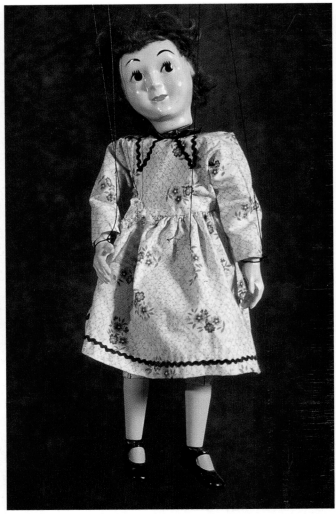

Jack: No. 705; Vinyl head and hands; 1962; $40-60. (Author's Collection)

Penny: No. 810; 1962; $40-60. (Author's Collection)

Left: Teto: No. 801; According to Hazelle's, their all-time bestseller; $50-75. (Author's Collection)

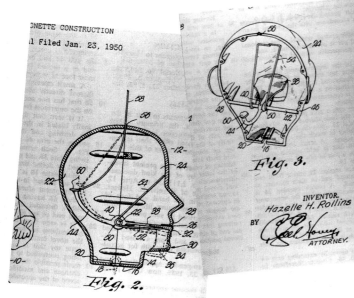

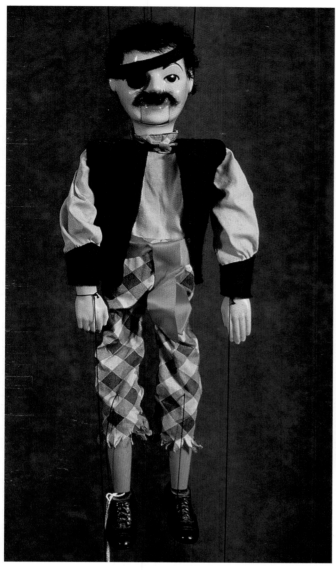

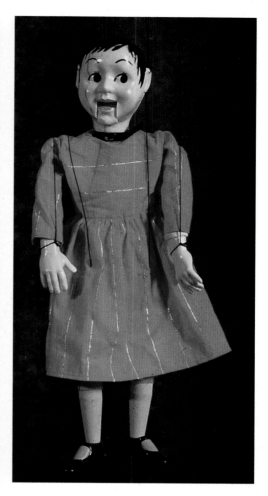

Nanette: Note original painted hair;
$40-60. (Author's Collection)

Pirate: No. 309; 1962; $50-75. (Author's Collection)

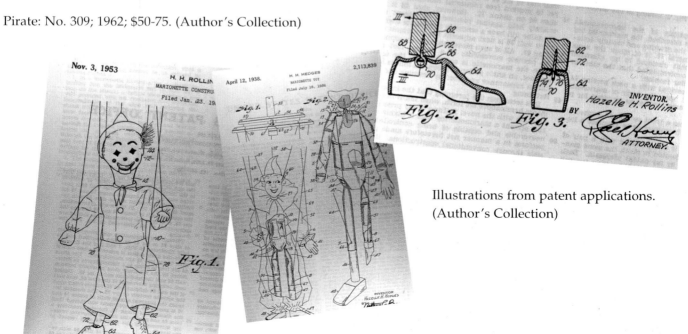

Illustrations from patent applications.
(Author's Collection)

Encore!

animals

Nearly all of the companies that have made marionettes have included animal characters, too. Constructed using a variety of combinations of wood, vinyl, rubber, wool, felt, and composition, animal marionettes can be as interesting as their names. For example, Bengo, Woofie, Honey Bear, Rupert, Iz, and Oz are a few. Sought by collectors, these dogs, bears, and even birds are considered prizes when found. Pelham Puppets had the most varied selection of animals available. Pelham Puppets' menagerie also included pigs, fish, snakes, calves, and caterpillars. A common mistake is the frequent misidentification of Pelham Puppets' cat as being Geppeto's cat, Figaro. Cyrus, a horse, made by Tony Sarg/Madame Alexander is a marionette character which is somewhat rare, as is Pet Pup, made by Virginia Austin. Both marionettes were made during the 1930s.

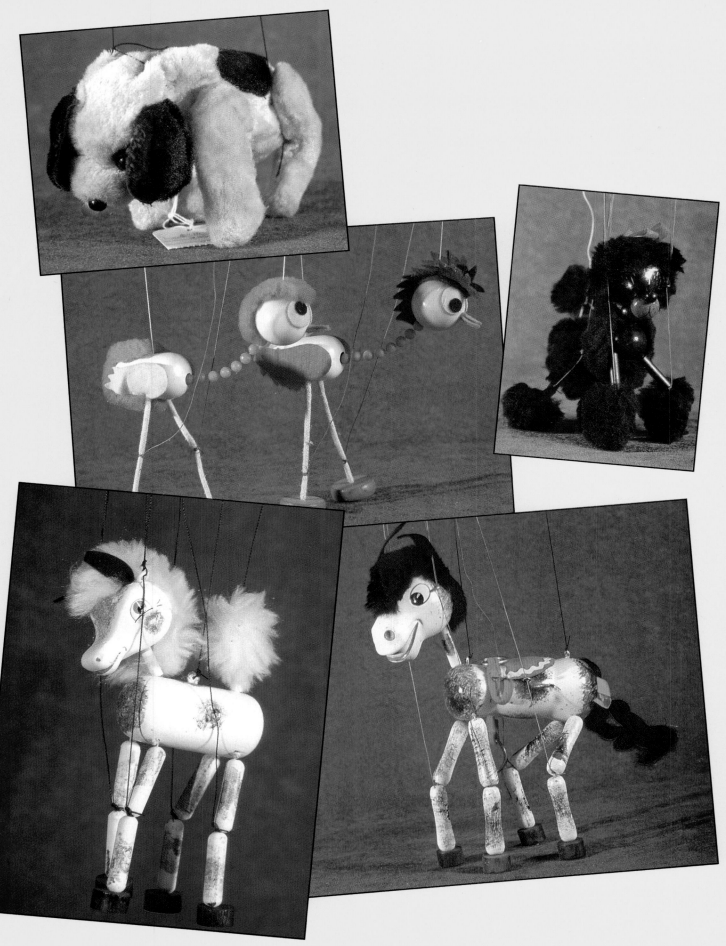

Helen Haiman Joseph

Helen Haiman Joseph was a prominent professional puppeteer during the 1920s and 1930s. She was adept at performing with various puppet forms, including hand and marionette puppets. Helen Haiman Joseph authored a number of

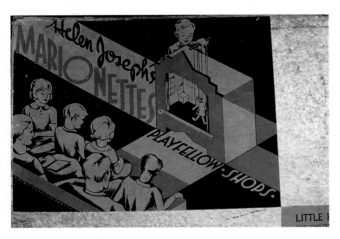

books on puppetry as well as the book titled *A Book Of Marionettes* written in the 1920s and published in New York. In 1936, she addressed the first American Puppetry Conference which was held in Detroit. The subject of her speech was the importance of hand puppets as a respectable puppetry form. Other well-known puppeteers in attendance at the conference included: Tony Sarg, Remo Bufano, Paul McPharlin, and Marjorie Batchelder.

For a short time during the 1930s, Helen Haiman Joseph designed and created commercially available marionettes. These marionettes have composition heads with painted features. The bodies consist of wood blocks, and the hands and feet are of shaped wood. The control is a simple wood T design and controls the puppet through five strings. Plain and almost crudely made, these marionettes are approximately 8 inches tall. One storybook box set contains the four characters of the *Little Red Riding Hood* story: Red Riding Hood, the Grandmother, the Wolf, and the Woodsman.

Box: Detail of 4-character Red Riding Hood box set; 1930s; $175-225 set. (Carmen & Gary Busk Collection)

Woodsman: Composition head; Wood hands and feet; One of four puppets included in a boxed set; 1930s; $30-50. (Carmen & Gary Busk Collection)

Grandmother: Composition head; Wood hands and feet; One of four puppets included in a boxed set; 1930s; $30-50. (Carmen & Gary Busk Collection)

Red Riding Hood: Composition head; Wood hands and feet; One of four puppets included in a boxed set; 1930s; $30-50. (Carmen & Gary Busk Collection)

Wolf (*Little Red Riding Hood*):
Composition head; Wooden hands and
feet; One of four puppets included in a
boxed set; 1930s; $30-50. (Carmen &
Gary Busk Collection)

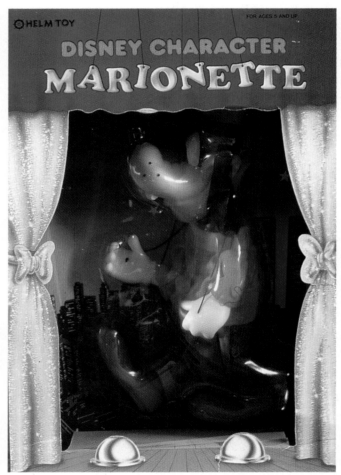

Helm Toys

In production only a short time, Helm Toys was licensed by the Walt Disney Company to make a group of popular Disney character marionettes. Goofy, Donald Duck, Mickey Mouse, and Minnie Mouse marionettes were sold by Helm Toys in 1990.

Helm Toys marionettes are made of plastic. They have molded features and stand approximately 16 inches tall. The marionette boxes are marked "The Walt Disney Co., Helm Toys, 1990, made in China."

Donald Duck: Box marked "The Walt Disney Company. Made in China. 1990"; $25-40. (Carmen & Gary Busk Collection)

Goofy: Box marked "The Walt Disney Company. Made in China. 1990"; $25-40. (Carmen & Gary Busk Collection)

Mickey Mouse: Box marked "The Walt Disney Company. Made in China. 1990"; $25-40. (Carmen & Gary Busk Collection)

Minnie Mouse: Box marked "The Walt Disney Company. Made in China. 1990"; $25-40. (Carmen & Gary Busk Collection)

Homemade

Homemade marionettes are just that—marionette characters made in the home. These puppets should not be automatically dismissed from being collected based on not being commercially produced. Many times, the construction of homemade marionettes incorporates designs and techniques also used on commercially made marionettes.

Homemade marionettes are made with almost innumerable materials, wood, composition, plaster, wax, latex, wire, even electrical tape. The optimum height for homemade puppets depends on the maker's fancy, examples from one inch to several feet tall are available. The controls of the homemade marionettes can vary also from a simple strip of wood to a myriad of detachable control bars and stops. The dress of the homemade puppet can vary, likewise, from a plain piece of cloth fashioned like a garment to an ornately festooned gown.

Since the early 1900s, dozens of books on do-it-yourself marionette making have been published. Many authored by well-known puppeteers such as Helen Haiman Joseph, Tony Sarg, and Remo Bufano. These books have often served as the starting point for marionettes made in the home.

Old Woman: Detail of homemade puppet. (Author's Collection)

Old Woman: Homemade puppet. $25-35. (Author's Collection)

Japan

During the late 1950s and early 1960s, a number of companies began producing character marionettes which were (in looks) similar to the then popular Pelham Puppets marionettes. These "knockoff" marionettes are identified (when they're marked) by a single small paper label which states "Japan," affixed to the control of the puppet.

Though similar in look to Pelhams, these made-in-Japan marionettes were constructed using lower quality materials. Lower quality body part molds, plastic body parts with molded blemishes, and use of string in the puppet's joints are some of the more obvious examples of lack of quality. Like Pelham, these "knock-off" marionettes have colored strings which correspond with like colored plastic bushings on the X-shaped control. Pinocchio, Pinky and Perky the Pig, and a horse were among the more popular characters to be copied by the Japanese marionette makers.

Because of the lower quality of construction, these "knockoff" marionettes were easily broken. Pelham Puppets suffered a great deal of bad press due to these marionettes which looked like real Pelhams. Legal action was initiated by Pelham Puppets against the companies selling these Japanese-made "knockoffs" and, in time, production of these marionettes was stopped.

Bear: Pelham Puppets knockoff; "Japan" sticker on controls; Composition head; Plastic hands; String joints; 1960s; $20-30. (Carmen & Gary Busk Collection)

Dog and Horse: Pelham Puppets knockoffs; "Japan" sticker on controls; 1960s; $20-30. (Carmen & Gary Busk Collection)

Kariudo: Hard plastic and cloth; Tag marked "I am Kariudo Hunter"; 1960s; $20-30. (Carmen & Gary Busk Collection)

Santa: Ceramic-type head and boots; "Japan" sticker on control; 1960s; $30-50. (Carmen & Gary Busk Collection)

Knickerbocker

The Knickerbocker Toy Company was another long-time established doll and toy maker that sold marionettes. Knickerbocker sold marionettes from the late 1950s through the early 1970s. Their marionettes were essentially stock 9- to 12-inch character dolls with strings and a control attached. Knickerbocker hand puppets share many of the same body components as their marionette counterparts. Knickerbocker marionettes usually have stuffed cloth bodies, and depending on the character, the head, hands, and feet could be made either of stuffed cloth or vinyl or rubber. On those puppets that did have vinyl or rubber body parts, the parts were painted or molded.

Knickerbocker marionettes have tags sewn into the body of the puppet. These tags have the name of the character, copyright or trademark information, the country in which the marionette was made, and year made (note: the year was not listed on all puppets). Earlier Knickerbocker marionettes were made in Japan, and later marionettes were made in Taiwan.

The controls are plastic and were marketed as "push button." The control has a pistol-type grip design. Movement was controlled through four levers (the "push buttons") which allowed for only a minimal range of motion for the marionette's arms and legs. Due to the material used and the fragility of its design, Knickerbockers' marionette controls were prone to break.

Simon: 11 inches tall; Cloth body; Tag marked "The Chipmunks Alvin - Simon - Theodore 1963"; $20-30. (Author's Collection)

Winnie Witch: Vinyl head, cloth body; Tag marked "Winnie Witch Knickerbocker Toy Company Inc. 1965, Made in Japan"; $20-30. (Author's Collection)

Raggedy Ann: Tag marked "Knickerbocker Toy Company made in Taiwan"; $40-60. (Carmen & Gary Busk Collection)

Bozo the Clown: Cloth body; Tag marked "Capitol Records Inc. Larry Harmon Picture Corp. Licensed Don Gardner Assoc. Inc."; $25-40. (Carmen & Gary Busk Collection)

Details from 1964 Sears Christmas Wishbook. (Carmen & Gary Busk Collection)

Kohner Brothers, Inc.

Kohner Brothers, Inc., of East Patterson, New Jersey, sold miniature Disney character marionettes during the early 1970s. These novelty puppets marketed as "Peppy Puppets" are made of hard plastic and vary in height from 4 to 5 inches. These marionettes were made in Hong Kong. In 1970, these marionettes were packaged in colorful cardboard boxes. By 1973, they were sold in shrink bubble wrap packages. Each character is marked "Copyright Walt Disney Productions—Made in Hong Kong." The controls for these marionettes are simple plastic bars with a small loop; three strings support the puppet. The Disney characters available include Pinocchio, Donald Duck, Mickey Mouse, Goofy, and Pluto.

Another type of marionette sold by Kohner is the "Magic Glove Marionette." This marionette consists of a Disney character playing a xylophone. The puppet has each hand and its head attached by three strings to a child's size white glove. The glove serves as the marionette's control. Manipulation of the glove allows the puppet character to "play" the xylophone.

The "Magic Glove Marionette" is made of hard plastic and stands about 9 inches tall. The puppet itself is unmarked. The box is marked "Copyright Walt Disney—made in Hong Kong."

Mickey Mouse: Copyright Disney; 1973; $15-25. (Author's Collection)

Pinocchio: Copyright Disney; 1973; $15-25. (Author's Collection)

Donald Duck: Copyright Disney; 1973; $15-25. (Author's Collection)

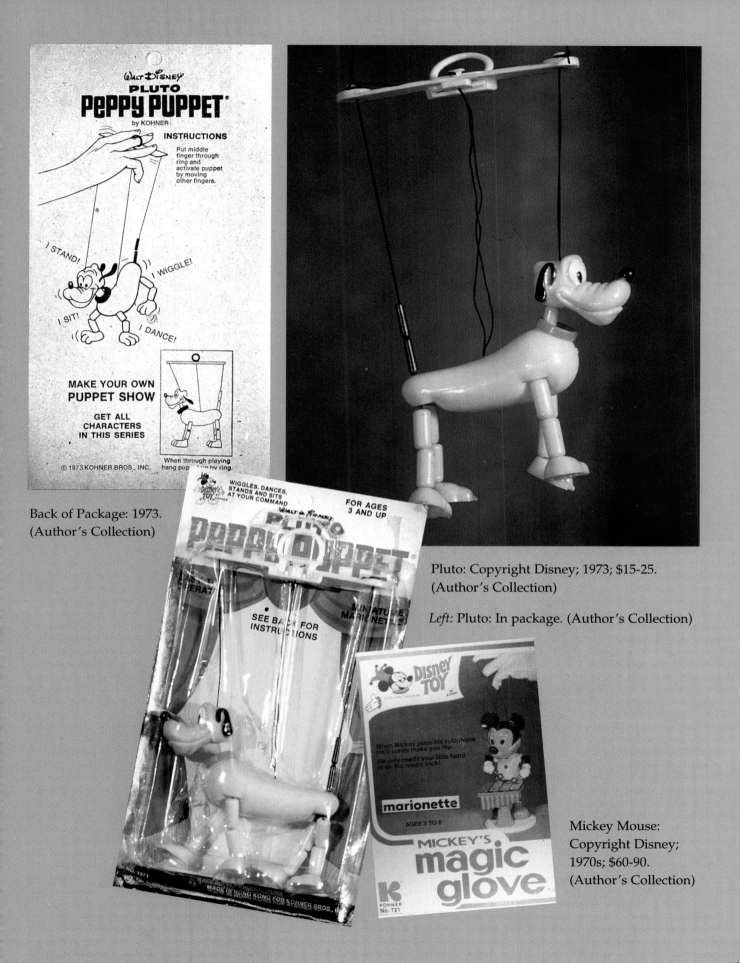

Back of Package: 1973.
(Author's Collection)

Pluto: Copyright Disney; 1973; $15-25.
(Author's Collection)

Left: Pluto: In package. (Author's Collection)

Mickey Mouse:
Copyright Disney;
1970s; $60-90.
(Author's Collection)

Kopy Kat

Based in Detroit, Michigan, the Wilson Inc. Company produced marionette educational kits during the late 1930s. Their Kopy Kat marionettes included a girl and a boy character.

Kopy Kat's educational kits contained the unfinished plaster puppet parts for two marionettes (for both a girl and a boy), paint, fabric, string, and wood for the controls. When assembled and finished, Kopy Kat marionettes are approximately 5 to 6 inches tall.

Detail of instructions for assembly. (Carmen & Gary Busk Collection)

Girl: Chalkware; 5 inches tall; $45-60. (Carmen & Gary Busk Collection)

Boy: Chalkware; 5 inches tall; $45-60. (Carmen & Gary Busk Collection)

Box Cover: Marked "Wilson Inc. Detroit Mich. 1937"; $90-125 set. (Carmen & Gary Busk Collection)

Madison Ltd.

Between 1977 and 1979 Madison Ltd., of Hackensack, New Jersey, sold a number of marionette characters. Wonder Woman, Superman, and Batman were the characters licensed from DC Comics. Disney granted a license to produce Goofy, Donald Duck, Minnie Mouse, and Mickey Mouse character marionettes. Madison Ltd. also created Donny and Marie Osmond character marionettes. The latter were somewhat rare, as fewer of the Osmond puppets were sold compared to the Disney and DC Comics characters.

Depending on the character, Madison Ltd., marionettes vary in height from approximately 10 to 15 inches. The controls are plastic as are the marionettes. The Disney characters are marked "Disney Productions - made in Hong Kong." The Madison Ltd., Disney marionette boxes are marked "Walt Disney Products, Jaymar Specialty Co. Madison Ltd., Hackensack New Jersey, made in Hong Kong."

Goofy: Copyright Disney; 1977-1979; $40-70. (Carmen & Gary Busk Collection)

Mickey Mouse: Copyright Disney; 1977-1979; $40-70. (Carmen & Gary Busk

Donald Duck: Copyright Disney; 1977-1979; $40-70. (Carmen & Gary Busk Collection)

Box (back): 1977-1979. (Carmen & Gary Busk Collection)

Box: Close-up of controls; 1977-1979. (Carmen & Gary Busk Collection)

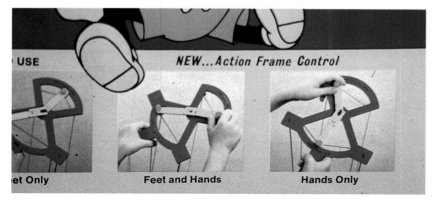

Detail of display unit. (Carmen & Gary Busk Collection)

Left and Opposite Page: Superman: Copyright DC Comics; Motorized Super Heroes display unit; late 1970s; $175-225. (Carmen & Gary Busk Collection)

ENCORE!
clowns

"Everybody loves a clown"—or so the saying goes. In the world of marionettes and string puppets, the saying rings true—as is evident from the variety of clown characters available from nearly all of the companies that sold marionettes. From white-faced clowns to black-faced minstrels, with names like Teto, Mario, Bimbo, and Clarabelle—clowns have won the hearts of millions of people. Hazelle's all-time best-selling marionette character was Teto the Clown. Pelham Puppets' most sought after clown goes by the name of Bimbo. So, as the lyrics from the Broadway musical, *A Little Night Music*, say, "Send in the Clowns."

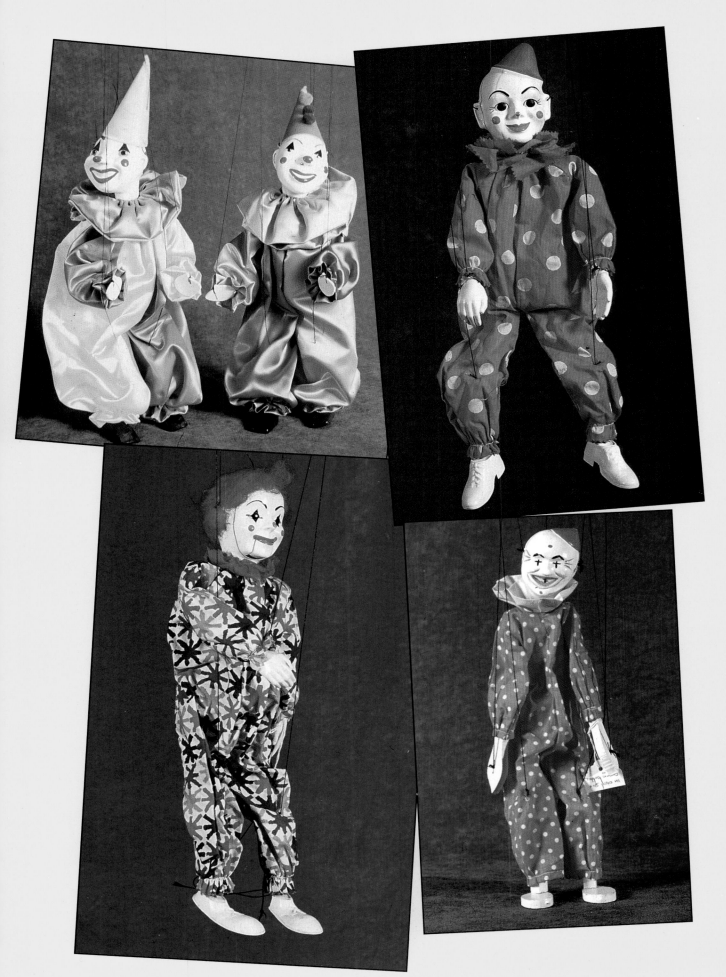

Pelham Puppets

Another familiar name in marionettes is Pelham Puppets. Spanning some six decades of marionette making, Pelham Puppets are known the world over. This British company was started in 1947 by Bob Pelham in Marlborough Wilts, England. Bob Pelham introduced hundreds of marionette, hand and ventriloquist puppet characters until his premature death in June of 1980. The Pelham Company remained in the Pelham family until 1986. Between 1986 and 1993, Pelham Puppets changed ownership three more times before officially closing its doors in March of 1993.

Production of "hand-made" puppets was a hallmark of the Pelham company. From the assembly of their bodies and the making of their clothing to the painting of each individual puppet face, each production process was completed by hand throughout.

The existence of Pelham Puppets was challenged during the early 1960s. A devastating fire in October of 1961 nearly wiped out the company, as several buildings were burnt to the ground. Some of the production materials and many finished puppets ready to ship, were saved from the fire. Lost, however, was a collection of nearly all of the original puppets which had been housed in Bob Pelham's office. The fire presented another opportunity for Bob Pelham to test his creative mettle in finding a way to resume production of his puppets. He accomplished this feat by moving his production line into improvised government surplus

Detail of pre-1970s metal disk knee joint. (Author's Collection)

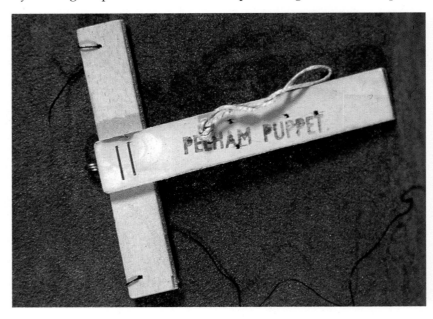

Early "T"-style controls: Ink stamped "Pelham Puppet"; Plywood; late 1940s. (Carmen & Gary Busk Collection)

Plastic Foot Joint: 1970s. (Carmen & Gary Busk Collection)

Detail of 1970s catalog. (Carmen & Gary Busk Collection)

Detail of 1970s catalog. (Carmen & Gary Busk Collection)

Detail of 1970s catalog. (Carmen & Gary Busk Collection)

Detail of 1970s catalog. (Carmen & Gary Busk Collection)

Detail of 1970s catalog. (Carmen & Gary Busk Collection)

Detail of 1970s catalog. (Carmen & Gary Busk Collection)

Detail of 1970s catalog. (Carmen & Gary Busk Collection)

Detail of 1970s catalog. (Carmen & Gary Busk Collection)

Detail of 1970s catalog. (Carmen & Gary Busk Collection)

Detail of 1970s catalog. (Carmen & Gary Busk Collection)

Detail of 1970s catalog. (Carmen & Gary Busk Collection)

Detail of 1970s catalog. (Carmen & Gary Busk Collection)

huts set up after the fire, and through having much of the hand work required to produce the puppets finished at the homes of his employees.

When purchasing Pelham Puppets, the new puppet owner was invited to join Pelpups, Pelham's official puppet club. In 1951, a newsletter call *Pelpup News* was created. This newsletter was one of the benefits of club membership. *Pelpup News* was a vehicle for Bob Pelham, known to the Pelpup members as Pelpop, to encourage and promote puppetry. Each issue included Pelpop's answers to club members' questions regarding puppets and puppetry. Also included were puppet plays, hints for performing with Pelham puppets, and other puppet-related stories.

The various abbreviations (SS, SL, JC, A, SM, etc., used along with the characters' name) do not have significance. They were used by the company for stock-keeping purposes, a way of keeping track of, and categorizing, their different puppet types.

To determine the age of Pelham marionettes, look for the following clues: Pelham Puppets' puppet heads are made of a molded pumice composition material or wood ball. Pre-1949 puppets do not have true round heads, as each puppet head was hand turned on a lathe with the resulting shapes leaning toward ovals or squarish rounds.

Pre-1950 puppet hands are made either from shaped wood or cast lead. From 1950 until 1970, the hands were made of composition. Plastic hands replaced the composition hands in the 1970s.

Knee joints made prior to 1950 were made of wood. Metal disk joints replaced the wood knee joints and continued to be used until the 1970s, when they were replaced by plastic. Wood arms and legs were used until the late 1960s, although plastic legs were used for certain characters as early as 1960.

Detail from 1980s catalog. (Carmen & Gary Busk Collection)

Detail of 1970s catalog. (Carmen & Gary Busk Collection)

OLD MAN

Detail from 1980s catalog. (Carmen & Gary Busk Collection)

Detail from 1980s catalog. (Carmen & Gary Busk Collection)

Detail from 1992 catalog. (Carmen & Gary Busk Collection)

Detail from 1980s catalog. (Carmen & Gary Busk Collection)

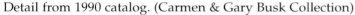

Detail from 1990 catalog. (Carmen & Gary Busk Collection)

The very first design for controls used by Pelham were a non-movable T-shape and were made from one-inch plywood. This design was replaced with the more commonly recognized "scissoring X" style. Black strings were used until 1955, when colored strings were employed. The colored strings correspond to like colored rubber bushings of the string guides on the controls, which were a part of the "tangle proof" control design patented by Pelham Puppets.

Pelham Puppets created original characters as well as popular television and radio characters from both England and the United States. Pelham obtained rights and began to produce Disney characters in 1953. Hanna-Barbera cartoon characters including Huckleberry Hound, Yogi Bear, and the Flintstones were put into production in the late 1950s.

In 1979, Pelham Puppets was granted rights to produce Charles Schultz's Peanuts characters, Charlie Brown, Snoopy, and Woodstock. The final major character series made by Pelham Puppets were those of the Thunderbirds.

Detail from 1992 catalog. (Carmen & Gary Busk Collection)

Detail from 1992 catalog. (Carmen & Gary Busk Collection)

Detail from 1992 catalog. (Carmen & Gary Busk Collection)

Detail from 1992 catalog. (Carmen & Gary Busk Collection)

Detail from 1992 catalog. (Carmen & Gary Busk Collection)

Detail from 1992 catalog. (Carmen & Gary Busk Collection)

Box Cover: With flying pig logo; late 1940s, very early 1950s. (Carmen & Gary Busk Collection)

Boxes. (Author's Collection)

Box. (Carmen & Gary Busk Collection)

Woodstock: Type SL; 1979; $60-80.
(Carmen & Gary Busk Collection)

Charlie Brown: Type SL;
1979; $95-125. (Carmen &
Gary Busk Collection)

Prince Charming and Cinderella: Type SL; 1970s; $60-80 each. (Carmen & Gary Busk Collection)

Cinderella: Type SL; 1960s; $60-80. (Author's Collection)

Mitzi(s): Type SS; 1970s (left); 1960s (right); $60-80 each. (Carmen & Gary Busk Collection)

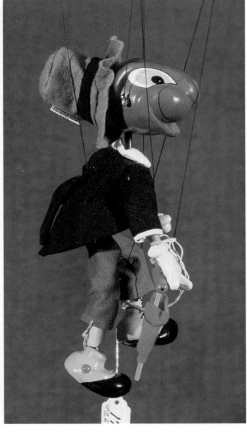

Jiminy Cricket: $150-200.
(Author's Collection)

Pinocchio(s): Note pinker coloring and marbled legs
of puppet on left; 1960s; $100-150. (Carmen & Gary
Busk Collection)

Pinocchio: Note pinker coloring and marbled legs.
(Carmen & Gary Busk Collection)

Pinocchio: Type SL; 1960s; $95-125.
(Author's Collection)

Geppeto: Type SL; 1970s; $70-90. (Carmen & Gary Busk Collection)

Santa Claus: Note the same head used for Geppeto puppet; 1970s; $70-90. (Carmen & Gary Busk Collection)

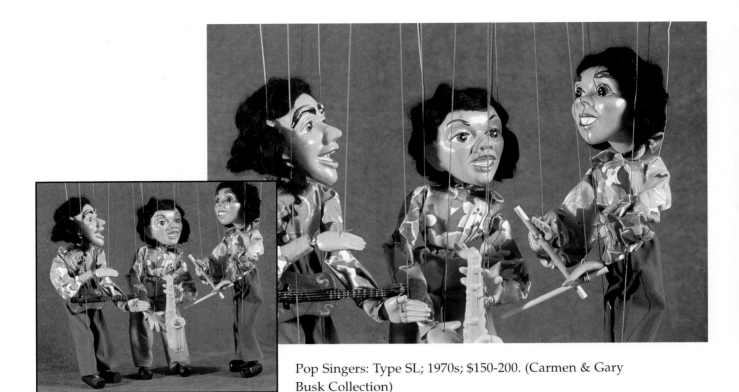

Pop Singers: Type SL; 1970s; $150-200. (Carmen & Gary Busk Collection)

Pop Singers: Type SL; 1970s; $150-200. (Carmen & Gary Busk Collection)

Pop Singer/Guitar Player: Type SL; 1970s; $150-200. (Carmen & Gary Busk Collection)

Pop Singer/Drummer: Type SL; Floral shirt; 1970s; $150-200. (Carmen & Gary Busk Collection)

Baby Dragon: Type A; 1970s. (Carmen & Gary Busk Collection)

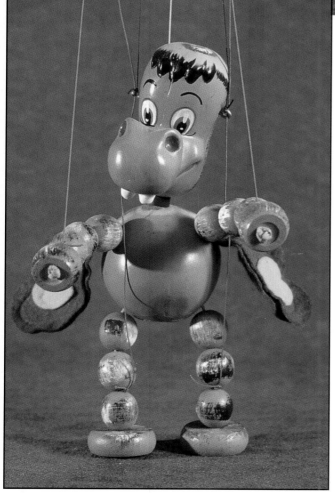

Mother Dragon: Type A; 1970s; $200-250. (Carmen & Gary Busk Collection)

Baby Dragon: Type A; 1970s; $150-200. (Carmen & Gary Busk Collection)

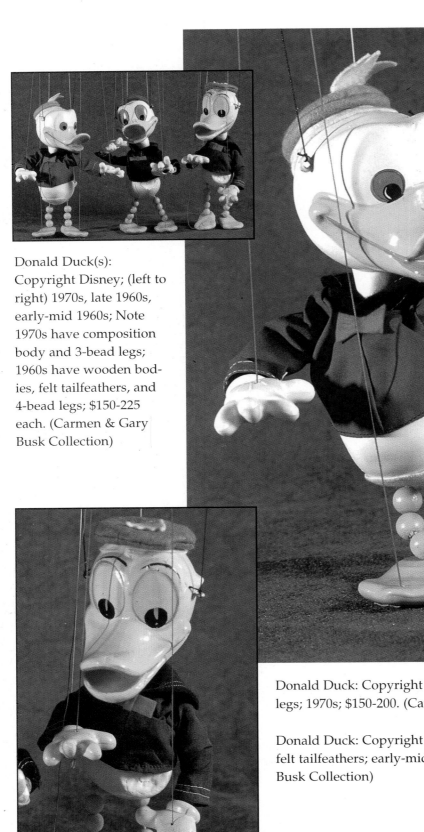

Donald Duck(s): Copyright Disney; (left to right) 1970s, late 1960s, early-mid 1960s; Note 1970s have composition body and 3-bead legs; 1960s have wooden bodies, felt tailfeathers, and 4-bead legs; $150-225 each. (Carmen & Gary Busk Collection)

Donald Duck: Copyright Disney; Has molded body; Note 3-bead legs; 1970s; $150-200. (Carmen & Gary Busk Collection)

Donald Duck: Copyright Disney; Note 4-bead legs; Wood body, felt tailfeathers; early-mid 1960s; $175-225. (Carmen & Gary Busk Collection)

Hansel: Type SL; Note plastic hands; 1970s; $60-80. (Author's Collection)

Gretel: Type SL; Note plastic hands; 1970s; $60-80. (Carmen & Gary Busk Collection)

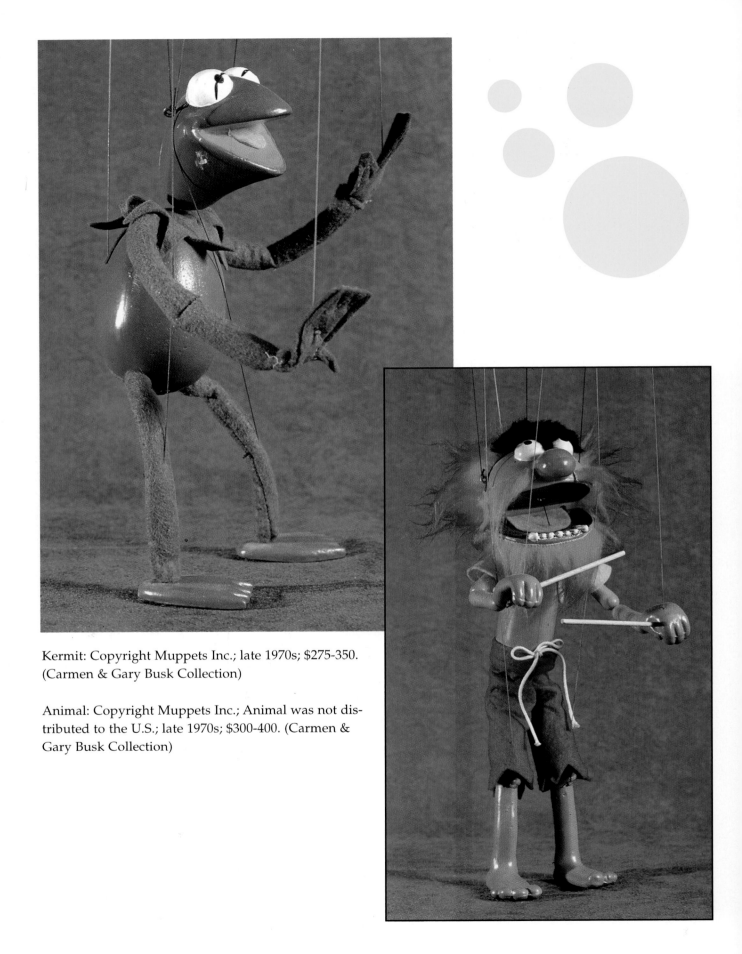

Kermit: Copyright Muppets Inc.; late 1970s; $275-350. (Carmen & Gary Busk Collection)

Animal: Copyright Muppets Inc.; Animal was not distributed to the U.S.; late 1970s; $300-400. (Carmen & Gary Busk Collection)

King and Queen: 1970s. (Carmen & Gary Busk Collection)

King and Queen: Type SL; 1970s; $90-125 each. (Carmen & Gary Busk Collection)

Bimbo the Clown: Type SL; 1970s; $90-125. (Carmen & Gary Busk Collection)

MacBoozle(s): (left to right) 1990s, 1970s; and a 1940s MacAwful the Scot (Talentoy). (Carmen & Gary Busk Collection)

MacBoozle(s): (left to right) 1990s, 1970s; Note socks, height, and nose differences; $60-80 each. (Carmen & Gary Busk Collection)

MacBoozle: 1990s; $60-80. (Carmen & Gary Busk Collection)

Above: Mickey and Minnie Mouse: Type SL; 1970s; $185-225. (Carmen & Gary Busk Collection)

Above Left: Mickey Mouse: Type SL; $185-225. (Carmen & Gary Busk Collection)

Left: Goofy: Type SL; 1970s; $125-150. (Carmen & Gary Busk Collection)

Daisy: Country Friends set; late 1980s; $30-50. (Carmen & Gary Busk Collection)

Ballet Dancer: Type SL; 1960s; $70-90. (Author's Collection)

Clown: Type SS; 1970s; $40-60. (Carmen & Gary Busk Collection)

Boy: Type SM; $70-90. (Carmen & Gary Busk Collection)

Dutch Girl: Type SS; 1970s; $40-60.
(Carmen & Gary Busk Collection)

Devil: Type SM; 1970s; $60-80. (Author's Collection)

Elephant: Type SL; 1970s; $90-125. (Author's Collection)

Fairy: Type SL; 1970s; $70-90. (Carmen & Gary Busk Collection)

Frog: Type SL; 1970s; $80-100. (Author's Collection)

Girl: Type SM; 1970s; $70-90. (Carmen & Gary Busk Collection)

Foal: Type A; 1970s; $60-90. (Author's Collection)

Horse: Type A; 1970s; $60-90. (Carmen & Gary Busk Collection)

Gypsy: Type SS; 1970s; $60-80. (Carmen & Gary Busk Collection)

Harlequin: 1980s; $70-90. (Carmen & Gary Busk Collection)

Indian Boy: Type SS; 1970s; $60-90. (Carmen & Gary Busk Collection)

Iz and Oz: Oz has blue head crest; 1970s; $40-60. (Carmen & Gary Busk Collection)

Mrs. Oblige/Old Woman: Type SM; 1970s; $60-80. (Carmen & Gary Busk Collection)

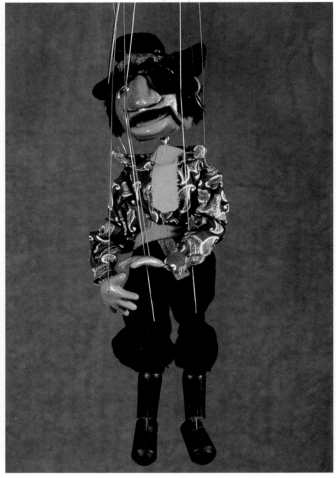

Pirate: Type SM; 1970s; $60-90. (Author's Collection)

Pluto: Type SL; 1970s; $135-175.
(Carmen & Gary Busk Collection)

Poodle: Type A; 1970s; $75-100. (Carmen & Gary Busk Collection)

Policeman: Type SS; 1970s; $75-100. (Carmen & Gary Busk Collection)

Red Riding Hood(s): Type SL; 1970s; $60-80. (Carmen & Gary Busk Collection)

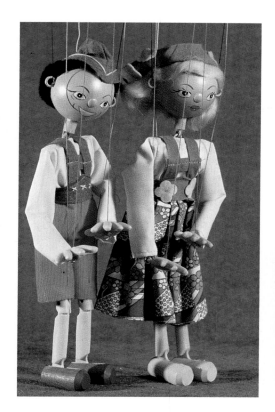

Tyroleon Boy and Tyroleon Girl: Type SS; 1970s; $60-80. (Carmen & Gary Busk Collection)

Sailor & Nurse: Type SS; 1970s; $60-80. (Carmen & Gary Busk Collection)

Rupert: Type SL; 1970s; $70-90. (Carmen & Gary Busk Collection)

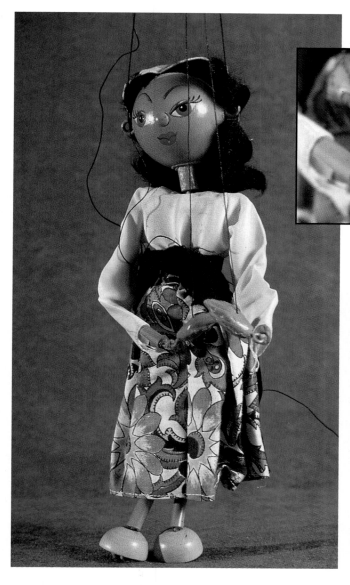

Dancing Girl: Detail of lead hands.
(Carmen & Gary Busk Collection)

Gypsy: Similar to an SS type in design, but on a JC type control; late 1940s; $100-150. (Carmen & Gary Busk Collection)

Wolf: Type SL; 1970s; $60-90.
(Author's Collection)

Fritzi and Mitzi: Type SS; 1970s; $60-80.
(Carmen & Gary Busk Collection)

Cowboy: Type SS; 1970s; $60-80. (Carmen & Gary Busk Collection)

Lulubelle: Type SS; approximately 24 inches tall; $175-250. (Carmen & Gary Busk Collection)

Golliwog: Type JC; 1970s; $125-175. (Carmen & Gary Busk Collection)

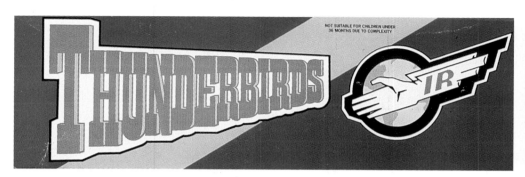

Thunderbirds Box Cover: Copyright ITC Entertainment Group; 1992. (Carmen & Gary Busk Collection)

Alan: Copyright ITC Entertainment Group; 1992; $125-175. (Carmen & Gary Busk Collection)

Lady Penelope: Copyright ITC Entertainment Group; Lady Penelope was made in two different costume versions; 1992; $125-175. (Carmen & Gary Busk Collection)

Parker: Copyright ITC Entertainment Group; 1992; $125-175. (Carmen & Gary Busk Collection)

Right: Brains: Copyright ITC Entertainment Group; 1992; $125-175. (Carmen & Gary Busk Collection)

Great Uncle Bulgaria: Character
from 1970s British television show.
(Carmen & Gary Busk Collection)

Wellington: Character from 1970s British television show; $125-175. (Carmen & Gary Busk Collection)

Bungo: Character from 1970s British television show; $125-175. (Carmen & Gary Busk Collection)

Tomsk: Character from 1970s British television show; $125-175. (Carmen & Gary Busk Collection)

Madame Cholet: Character from 1970s British television show; $125-175. (Carmen & Gary Busk Collection)

Orinoco: Type JC; 1970s; $125-175. (Carmen & Gary Busk Collection)

ENCORE!

disney

Disney may hold the record for creating the greatest number of memorable characters. Their images have set the standard by which storybook characters are recognized around the world. From Disney's first images of Mickey Mouse piloting a steamship, to the seven dwarfs peering into the face of a sleeping Snow White, to Alice visiting Wonderland, and to the Lady and the Tramp, Disney transforms a character's written description into a visual memory. These are but a few of the various interpretations of Disney characters made as marionettes.

Peter Puppet Playthings

Peter Puppet Playthings may best be known for their marionette characters from *The Howdy Doody Show.* Howdy Doody, Dilly Dally, Mr. Bluster, Clarabelle, Princess SummerFall-WinterSpring, two different versions of the Flub-A-Dub, and two lesser known Howdy Doody characters, Heidi Doody (Howdy's cousin) and Zippy the monkey.

Peter Puppet Playthings also offered a number of licensed Disney marionette characters and several original marionette characters, as well. Additional marionettes sold by Peter Puppet Playthings that originated from television programs included the twins Buzzy and Boopie, Lil' Mischief the Panda from *Big Brother,* Bob Emery's Small Fry Club, and a boy and girl mouseketeer marionette from Disney's *Mickey Mouse Club.* The character Merry Mailman was another marionette character originating from the television show, *The Merry Mailman.*

Alice: Detail from 1952 catalog. (Author's Collection)

Minnie Mouse: Detail from 1952 catalog. (Author's Collection)

Mickey Mouse: Detail from 1952 catalog. (Author's Collection)

According to New York State records, Peter Puppet Playthings was incorporated in April of 1947, some eight months before the first *Howdy Doody Show* aired on television. Peter Puppet Playthings marionettes were created and designed by Raye Copeland, to whom a patent was granted for his design of the "Unitrol" control for the marionette. This particular control design was to allow for complete control of the marionette character using only one hand. Peter Puppet Playthings marionettes were made at their factory in Long Island City, New York.

Peter Puppet Playthings marionettes have composition heads, hands, legs, and feet, and wood block bodies. In the mid-1950s, "jiggle" eyes started being used on some characters. Each puppet may be marked "PPP" or "P Puppet" on the lower rear base of the head. Some characters have no marks. Another clue in identifying Peter Puppet Playthings marionettes is by their distinctly shaped "Untitrol" controls. These are in the shape of a trapezoid and are made of black cardboard or plastic. Plastic was used in place of cardboard in the late 1950s.

In 1952, Peter Puppet Playthings introduced a new series of marionettes with professional-type controls. These puppets are larger than the standard puppets at 18 inches in height and have a wood control similar in design to Hazelle's patented airplane controls. Peter Puppet Playthings professional-type controls can be distinguished by a metal clip, which holds a removable cross-bar.

Detail from 1952 catalog. (Author's Collection)

Peter Puppet Playthings sold marionettes individually and in package sets. Package sets could include two or more marionette characters, one of a variety of stages, scripts, and admission tickets, with some sets including records. Among the package sets were Disney's *Alice in Wonderland*, *Peter Pan*, and *Pinocchio*. Other sets included Hansel and Gretel, and Cecil B. DeMille's, *The Greatest Show On Earth*.

Peter Puppet Playthings, Inc., was officially dissolved in December of 1962, after some 15 years of selling marionettes.

Pinocchio: Detail from 1952 catalog. (Author's Collection)

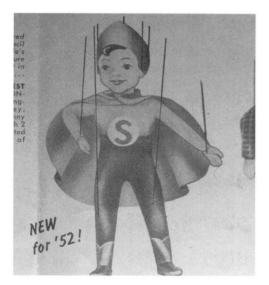

Space Man: Detail from 1952 catalog. (Author's Collection)

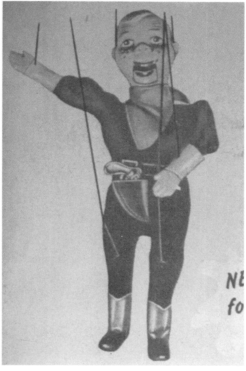

Cowboy: Detail from 1952 catalog. (Author's Collection)

Monkey: Detail from 1952 catalog. (Author's Collection)

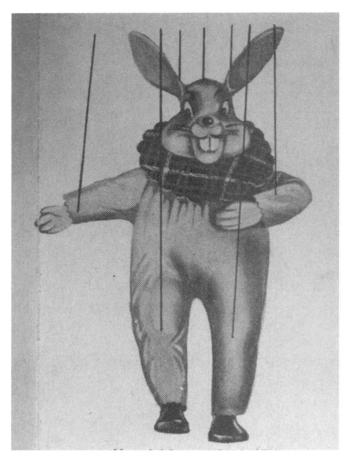

Bugsie: Detail from 1952 catalog. (Author's Collection)

Mario: Detail from 1952 catalog. (Author's Collection)

Patty: Detail from 1952 catalog.
(Author's Collection)

Peter: Detail from 1952 catalog.
(Author's Collection)

Tinkle Bear: Detail from 1952 catalog. (Author's Collection)

Bobo: Detail from 1952 catalog. (Author's Collection)

Sonya: Detail from 1952 catalog. (Author's Collection)

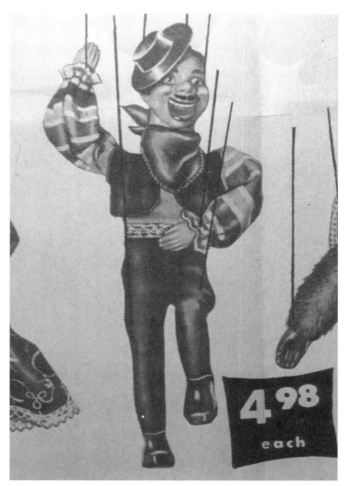

Chiquita: Detail from 1952 catalog; This could be Howdy in drag without freckles; The same mold was used for this marionette and the Howdy marionette. (Author's Collection)

Chico: Detail from 1952 catalog; Howdy sans freckles, with a mustache? (Author's Collection)

No. 705
WOOFIE — The Dog

6" Tall and 12" Long: He dances, sits up and begs, wags his tail . . . a perky bow on his head and fluffy fur ears.
Retail $4.98

Woofie: Detail from 1952 catalog. (Author's Collection)

Walt Disney's ALICE in WONDERLAND

IN WONDERLAND
ETE PACKAGED SHOW
ng Alice . . . Mad Hatter
March Hare Marionettes

A colorful stage with simple roll-up curtain. Everything necessary to put on a real marionette show. Unbreakable record with theme song from movie, plus tickets for admission. Two backdrop scenes for the children to color.
Retail $9.98

No. 370 — "ALICE" — in a pretty blue and

Alice in Wonderland Box Set: Set included Alice, Mad Hatter, March Hare, stage, record, and tickets; Detail from 1952 catalog. (Author's Collection)

Snow White: Detail from 1952 catalog. (Author's Collection)

Howdy Doody: Copyright Bob Smith; Howdy and original box; 1950s; $200-275. (Carmen & Gary Busk Collection)

Flub-a-Dub: Copyright Bob Smith; One of the two different styles of Flub-a-Dubs made by Peter Puppet Playthings; 1950s; $250-350. (Carmen & Gary Busk Collection)

Mr. Bluster: Copyright Bob Smith; 1950s; $300-400. (Carmen & Gary Busk Collection)

Clarabelle: Copyright Bob Smith; 1950s; $275-350. (Carmen & Gary Busk Collection)

Zippy: Copyright Bob Smith; Zippy was a real monkey who joined *The Howdy Doody Show* sometime during the 1953-1954 seasons; His tenure was not long, as he was prone to "freak out" and scream on the set; He was also known to bite cast members; $300 plus. (Carmen & Gary Busk Collection)

Minnie Mouse: Copyright Disney; 1950s; $150-200. (Carmen & Gary Busk Collection)

Princess SummerFall-WinterSpring: Copyright Bob Smith; Note the "jiggle" eyes; 1950s; $200-250. (Carmen & Gary Busk Collection)

Dilly Dally: Copyright Bob Smith; 1950s; $350-500. (Carmen & Gary Busk Collection)

Pinocchio: Copyright Disney; Note the "jiggle" eyes; mid-late 1950s; $150-200. (Carmen & Gary Busk Collection)

Alice in Wonderland: Copyright
Disney; 1950s; $75-150. (Carmen
& Gary Busk Collection)

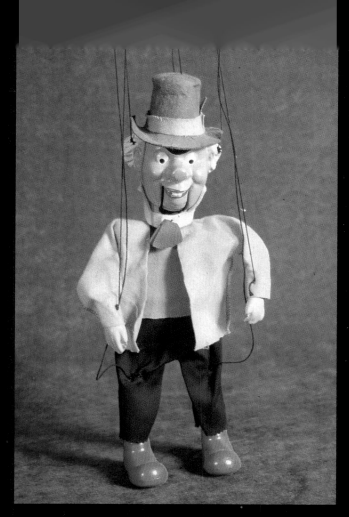

Mad Hatter: 1950s; $75-150. (Carmen & Gary Busk Collection)

March Hare: 1950s; $75-150. (Carmen & Gary Busk Collection)

Alice in Wonderland Box. (Carmen & Gary Busk Collection)

Indian: 1950s; $75-100. (Carmen & Gary Busk Collection)

Cowboy: 1950s; $75-100. (Carmen & Gary Busk Collection)

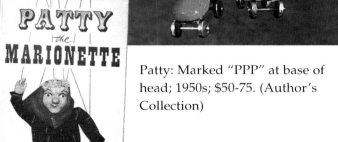

A BIG BROTHER
"Small Fry"
MARIONETTE

A PETER PUPPET PRODUCT

SIMPLE 'UNITROL' 1 HAND CONTROL
PAT. PEND

Boopie: The Small Fry Club; One of the twins from the *Big Brother* Bob Emery children's television show, which aired from March 1947 through June 1951 on Dumont Television; Boopie's twin brother's name is Buzzy; $50-75. (Author's Collection)

Small Fry Club Box: 1950s. (Carmen & Gary Busk Collection)

PATTY
the
MARIONETTE

THE NEW SKATING SENSATION

A PETER PUPPET PRODUCT

SIMPLE 'UNITROL' 1 HAND CONTROL
PAT. PEND

Patty: Marked "PPP" at base of head; 1950s; $50-75. (Author's Collection)

Patty Box. (Author's Collection)

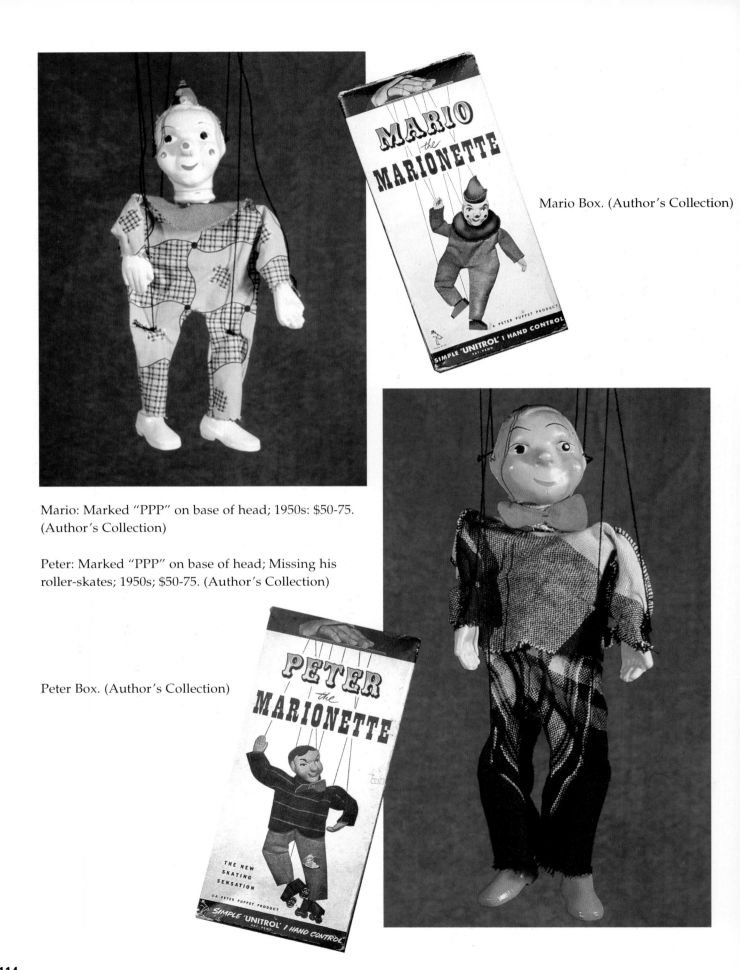

Mario Box. (Author's Collection)

Mario: Marked "PPP" on base of head; 1950s: $50-75. (Author's Collection)

Peter: Marked "PPP" on base of head; Missing his roller-skates; 1950s; $50-75. (Author's Collection)

Peter Box. (Author's Collection)

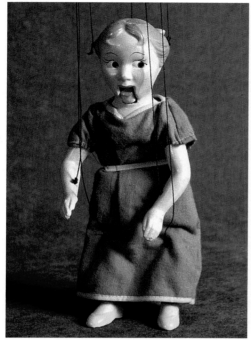

Wendy: Copyright Disney; 1950s; $100-150. (Carmen & Gary Busk Collection)

Peter Pan: Copyright Disney; Marked "PPP"; Note original knives; 1950s; $85-150. (Author's Collection)

Captain Hook: Copyright Disney; 1950s; $125-175. (Carmen & Gary Busk Collection)

Dopey: 1950s; $175-225.
(Carmen & Gary Busk Collection)

Snow White: One of their
"deluxe" puppets; 1950s;
$225-275. (Carmen & Gary
Busk Collection)

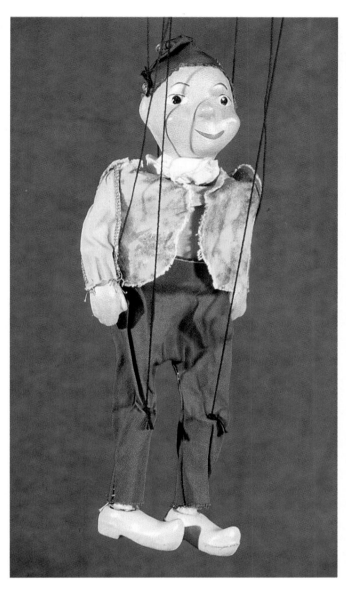

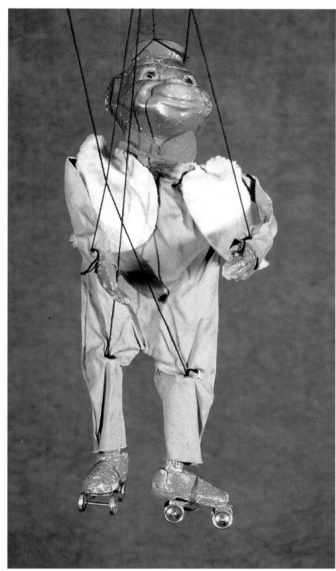

Hansel: 1950s; $40-60. (Author's Collection)

Monkey: 1950s; $30-50. (Author's Collection)

ENCORE!

ethnic characters

Since the 1930s, ethnic characters have been popular. American Crayon, Effanbee, Pelham Puppets, Shackman's, Hazelle's, Bob Baker, and Peter Puppet Playthings have all sold ethnic characters. Ethnic character marionettes are much sought after by collectors, and usually command higher retail and auction prices when compared with non-ethnic characters. Lucifer, designed by Virginia Austin, and sold by Effanbee during the 1930s, was originally sold barefoot. A later version, sold during the late 1930s, had Lucifer wearing shoes. The change was purportedly due to possible offensiveness of racial stereotyping. Hazelle's included a myriad of ethnic marionette characters over the years. This was not by chance, as Hazelle Hedges Rollins actively sought to expand children's understanding of ethnic differences and similarities through puppetry.

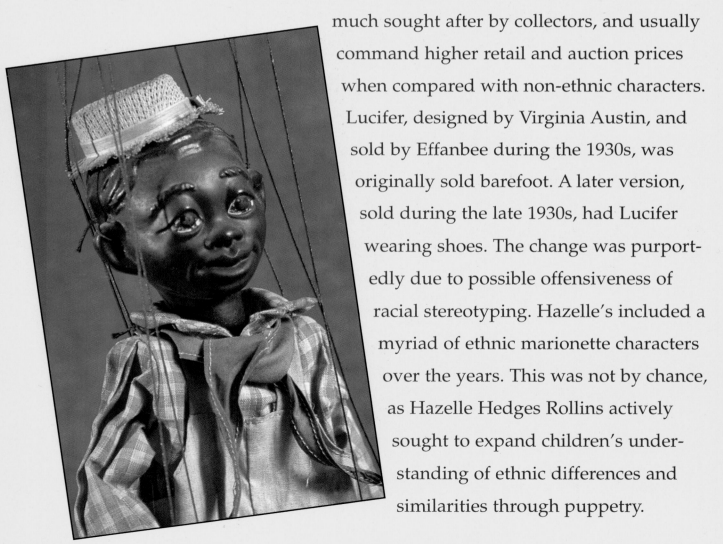

Pride Products Company

The Pride Products Company was in business only a few years from the late 1950s through the very early 1960s. Their most recognized marionette character was Howdy Doody. Pride Products marionettes have plastic heads, hands, and feet, and are approximately 14 inches tall. Some of the different characters have moving mouths and movable eyes. The creation of Pride Products Company may have been an attempt at reorganizing the then failing company of Peter Puppets Playthings.

Prince Charming: late 1950s; $100-125. (Carmen & Gary Busk Collection)

Howdy Doody: late 1950s; $200-230. (Carmen & Gary Busk Collection)

Cinderella: late 1950s; $100-125. (Carmen & Gary Busk Collection)

Schmiders

These marionettes were made in the Black Forest region in Germany during the early 1970s. Schmiders' marionettes have wood heads, hands, and feet, and are from 14 to 18 inches in height. Made using a process called "repli-carve," the head and hands are machine shaped with the end result looking as if the piece had been hand carved. Controls for Schmiders marionettes differ from most of the other commercially-made marionettes, as they are designed to be held vertically.

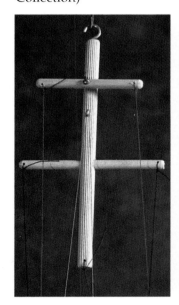

Harlekin: 1970s; $100-150. (Carmen & Gary Busk Collection)

Prinzessin: 1970s; $100-150. (Carmen & Gary Busk Collection)

Vertical Design Control: 1970s. (Carmen & Gary Busk Collection)

Woodsman: 1970s; $100-150. (Carmen & Gary Busk Collection)

Peppi: 1970s; $100-150. (Carmen & Gary Busk Collection)

Souvenir Marionettes

Made primarily in Mexico and sold as souvenirs—and also available as carnival midway prizes—these marionettes can date to the 1930s and 1940s. Souvenir marionettes have two distinctive features. The first is the seemingly consistent, crude construction of the puppet—from the tying of the strings to the marionette character, to the attachment of the clothes to the puppets using tacks, to the plastic "flash" of the molded body parts. The second distinctive feature is the shaped flat wood feet/shoes, which are nearly always painted some shade of red.

The characters depicted by these marionettes are most frequently Mexican banditos and senoritas, black minstrels, comic characters, and clowns. Bugs Bunny, Porky Pig, Mickey Mouse, Olive Oyl, and Batman are just a few of the unlicensed "knockoffs" made as souvenir marionettes.

Pre-1970s souvenir marionettes have plaster heads and hands, wood block bodies, molded and painted features, the flat red wood feet/shoes, and small crude fixed X-shaped controls. The female characters may have yarn, wool, or painted hair. Souvenir marionettes made in the 1970s and early 1980s have plaster heads and plastic hands. The puppets made from the mid-1980s and forward have plastic heads, hands, and plastic or resin feet and controls. When present, marks on these marionettes include the city and country of origin, for example "Perez Mexico," and are ink stamped on the bottom of either of the character's feet.

Mexican Man: Plaster head and hands, plastic gun; $15-30. (Author's Collection)

Mexican Man: Plaster head and hands, plastic gun, cardboard guitar. $15-30. (Author's Collection)

Mexican Man: Plaster head, hands, feet, and spangle eyes. $15-30. (Author's Collection)

Mexican Man: Plaster head and hands. $15-30.
(Author's Collection)

Mexican Man: Plaster head, hands, and feet. $15-30.
(Author's Collection)

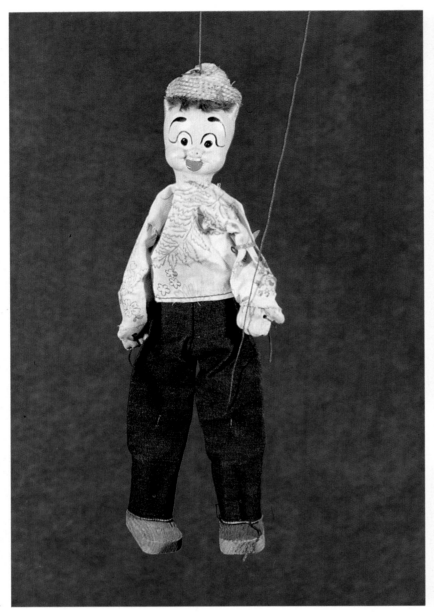

Porky Pig: Plaster head and hands; $15-30. (Author's Collection)

Mickey Mouse: Plaster head, plastic hands; $15-30. (Author's Collection)

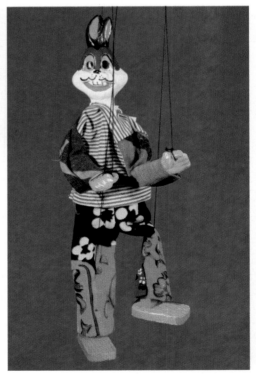

Bugs Bunny: Plaster head and hands; $15-30. (Author's Collection)

Mexican Woman: Plaster head and hands; $15-30.
(Author's Collection)

Talentoy

Talent Products, Inc., of 29 Fifth Street, New York, was comprised of two entities, Talentoy and Talentoon. In 1948, a set of five different Talentoy puppet characters, Pim Bo the Clown, Kilroy the Cop, Jambo the Jiver, MacAwful the Scot, and Toonga from the Congo, were distributed by the Effanbee Doll Company.

Talentoy puppets have round wood heads, wood block bodies, and rounded wood feet. The hands are made from cast lead. Talentoy puppets are approximately 12 inches tall. The eyes and mouths are applied decals as opposed to having painted features.

Each Talentoy puppet came with a set of operating instructions, which included a short biography of each particular puppet character. Also included with each puppet, a Talentoon 33-1/2 long play album which had songs and music for each puppet character and a sheet with the lyrics to the songs.

One may speculate that Talent Products purchased unfinished puppets from Pelham Puppets and finished them in the United States. The foundation for this speculation is based on similarities between the Talentoy puppets and their Pelham Puppets counterparts. Both the Talentoy and Pelham puppets have the round wood heads, use wood knee and ankle joints, have cast lead hands, and have the dowel-type feet. Talentoy has MacAwful the Scot; Pelham has MacBoozle. Talentoy has Toonga from the Congo; Pelham has Lulubelle; Talentoy has Pim Bo the Clown; Pelham has Clever Willie. Talentoy has Kilroy the Cop and Pelham has the Policeman.

MacAwful the Scot: Lead hands; Eyes and mouth are decals; $150-200. (Author's Collection)

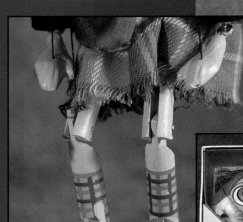

MacAwful the Scot: Detail of wood knee joint; 1948. (Carmen & Gary Busk Collection)

MacAwful the Scot in his original box. (Carmen & Gary Busk Collection)

126

Hours of Enchantment

We little people bring to children from 6 to 60 a hobby with limitless possibilities for home entertainment and **WE DEVELOP TALENT.** We stimulate imagination. We create interest in rhythm, in music and self expression. We develop finger dexterity and powers of coordination. Our phonograph record and a script that goes with it, make it easy to put on your first puppet show. After that, imagination and ingenuity take over! Any child over 6 can easily work us.

We puppets are wonderful little people.
Signed: Pin-Bo the Clown

Joonga from the Congo
Mac Awful the Scot
Kilroy the Cop
Jambo the Jiver

JAMBO THE JIVER

Jambo, Jambo, Jambo!

That's alright; don't repeat!
When I hear that boogie-beat,
I just hustle down the street
To give you folks a little treat
A-dancin'—with these walkie-talkie feet.

Now I'm a jitterbuggin' fool;
Although I never went to school.
So I can't write so very neat,
Because my spelling's with my feet.
But I can dance and dance again
A-while you're countin' up to ten.
So you just sit back in your seat
And let yourself relax complete,
A-while I git back on that beat.
Alright, professor, let me have it,
Reeeeet!

Now kick your feet and lift your feet.
Then change your feet and shift your feet
Keep 'em beating out that steady beat,
Yeah!

Jambo, Jambo, Jambo, Jambo,

Box Cover: 1948. (Carmen & Gary Busk Collection)

Jambo the Jiver: Eyes and mouth are applied decals; 1948; $175-225. (Author's Collection)

Jambo's Talentoon Song Lyrics. (Author's Collection)

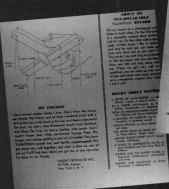

Jambo Paper Label: Stapled to Jambo's jacket. (Author's Collection)

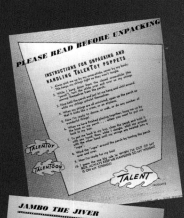

Talentoy and Jambo Instructions. (Author's Collection)

Record label for Jambo's Talentoon Record. (Author's Collection)

ENCORE!
pinocchio

Since C. Collodi first wrote the story of *Pinocchio* in the late 1880s, the terms "marionette" and "Pinocchio" have been nearly synonymous to people the world over. There have been almost as many different versions of Pinocchio made as there are adventures written about the stringed puppet. Perhaps the earliest-recognized version is that made popular in the animated Disney classic, *Pinocchio*. Regardless of the maker, nearly all of the Pinocchio characters share the familiar feathered hat, shorts outfit, and, of course, distinct nose.

Tony Sarg/Madame Alexander

Cellophane envelope: Envelope containing Tony Sarg marionette charm; early 1940s. (Author's Collection)

Master puppeteer Tony Sarg was America's pre-eminent puppet showman during the 1920s and the 1930s. His talents were many and his areas of interest were varied. He illustrated and authored numerous books ranging from adult non-fiction to children's books. Tony Sarg's business ventures were also far afield as they included jewelry, dolls, marionettes, and barbershops for children. Tony Sarg mentored dozens of puppeteers during the 1920s and 1930s. Many went on to prominent careers of their own. Rufus and Margo Rose later went on the *The Howdy Doody Show*. Harold Hestwood sold thousands of Mickey Mouse marionettes during the early 1930s in the Los Angeles area. Bill Baird created and performed the memorable "goatherd" marionette scene in the movie, *The Sound of Music*.

Tony Sarg created hundreds of marionette characters throughout the 1920s and the 1930s and entertained millions of people with his puppet creations and marionette productions. The largest (in physical size) marionette production accomplished by Tony Sarg was the design and creation of the first character balloons used in the Macy's Thanksgiving Day parade in 1928.

Tony Sarg's first commercially produced children's marionettes were made in Italy and were sold in the United States during the 1920s. During the 1930s, some forty different marionette characters were designed and created by Tony Sarg, and were manufactured by and distributed through the Alexander Doll Company. Many, but not all, of these marionettes are marked "Tony Sarg/Alexander" on the lower rear base of the character's head and/or on the upper back of the puppet. Some of Tony Sarg's marionettes are identified by a cloth tag with the character's name attached to the puppet's outfit or the puppet's wrist.

Depending on the marionette character, the majority of Tony Sarg's marionettes have composition heads, hands, and feet. These puppets vary in height from 8 to 14 inches. Many of the marionette characters use a Czech-style design where the puppet is suspended

Tweedle Dee: Tony Sarg marionette charm; early 1940s; $30-50. (Author's Collection)

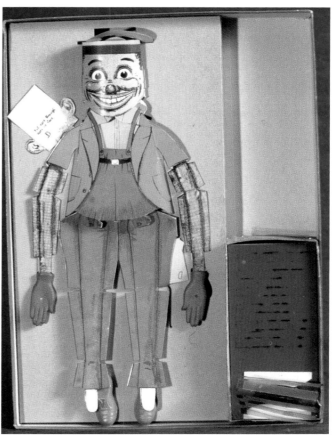

Hi Pockets: Box cover of cardboard marionette kit; 1940. (Carmen & Gary Busk Collection)

Hi Pockets: Three-dimensional cardboard body; Composition hands and shoes; $175-225. (Carmen & Gary Busk Collection)

by, and supported through, a main wire attaching the puppets to the controls.

The larger Disney marionettes made by Tony Sarg/Alexander came with a blue draw-string storage pouch. The Disney seven dwarfs came as a group and were packaged in one box. The dwarf Dopey was also available as a kit. Tony Sarg/Alexander also sold several different marionette theaters.

Marionette charms were another creation from Tony Sarg. These small charms have movable limbs and are painted in bright enamel colors. There are at least seven characters to this set including the *Alice in Wonderland* character Tweedle Dee. Each charm was packaged in small cellophane envelopes labeled "Tony Sarg Marionette Charm."

In 1940, the Selchow and Righter Company sold a set of Tony Sarg designed 3-dimensional cardboard marionette kits. These do-it-yourself marionette kits had composition hands and feet. The marionettes were assembled using tabs to attach the cardboard body and limbs to the rest of the body parts. Some of the characters in this series are Hi Pockets, Jitter Jack and Jitter Jill, Dipsey Doodle, and Willie Wiggle. Tony Sarg died in February of 1942.

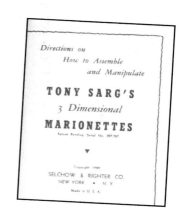

Assembly and manipulation instructions for three-dimensional marionette: Made by Selchow & Righter Co.; 1940. (Carmen & Gary Busk Collection)

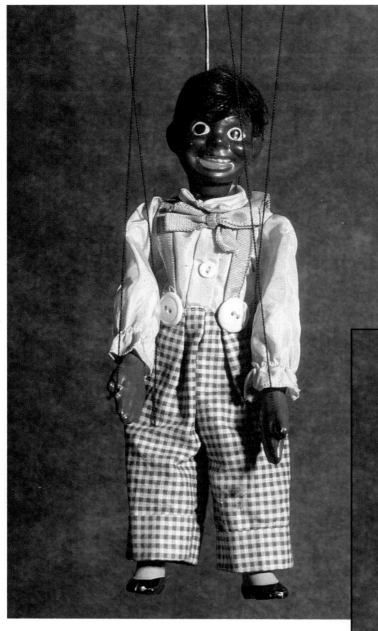

Sambo: *The Dixieland Minstrel* play; 1930s; $175-225.
(William Biskie Collection)

Bones: *The Dixieland Minstrel* play; 1930s; $175-225.
(William Biskie Collection)

The Dame: *Rip Van Winkle* play; 1930s; $125-175. (William Biskie Collection)

Interlocutor: *The Dixieland Minstrel* play; 1930s; $125-175. (William Biskie Collection)

Judith: *Rip Van Winkle* play; Missing original hat; 1930s; $125-175. (William Biskie Collection)

Bashful: Copyright Disney;
1930s; $200-300. (William
Biskie Collection)

Doc: Copyright Disney; 1930s; $200-300. (William Biskie Collection)

Grumpy: Copyright Disney; 1930s; $200-300. (William Biskie Collection)

Happy: Copyright Disney; 1930s; $200-300. (William Biskie Collection)

Dopey: Copyright Disney; Dopey was also available in kit form; 1930s; $250-350. (William Biskie Collection)

Snow White: Copyright Disney; $175-275. (William Biskie Collection)

Sleepy: Copyright Disney; 1930s; $200-300. (William Biskie Collection)

Disney Marionette Box Cover: Copyright Disney; All seven of the dwarfs were packaged in boxes like this. (William Biskie Collection)

Witch: Copyright Disney; *Hansel & Gretel* play; 1930s; $125-175. (William Biskie Collection)

Sneezy: Copyright Disney; 1930s; $200-300. (William Biskie Collection)

Prince Charming: Copyright Disney; *Snow White* play; 1930s; $175-225. (William Biskie Collection)

Top Right: Huntsman: Copyright Disney; His tag reads "Hunter"; 1930s; $200-250. (William Biskie Collection)

Right: Alice in Wonderland: Copyright Disney; In two plays, one with Dweedle Dee & Dum and one with Humpty Dumpty; 1930s; $150-225. (William Biskie Collection)

Humpty Dumpty: Copyright Disney; 1930s; $150-225. (William Biskie Collection)

Left: Tweedle Dee: Copyright Disney; 1930s; $150-225. (William Biskie Collection)

Margaret: *The Three Wishes* play; Note hole in nose for special effects in play. (William Biskie Collection)

Tweedle Dum: Copyright Disney; 1930s; $150-225. (William Biskie Collection)

Margaret: *The Three Wishes* play; 1930s; $125-175. (William Biskie Collection)

Martin: *The Three Wishes* play; 1930s; $125-175.
(William Biskie Collection)

Fairy Titania: *The Three Wishes* play; 1930s; $125-175.
(William Biskie Collection)

Fido the Dog: *Clever Gretchen* play; 1930s; $150-200. (William Biskie Collection)

Gretchen: *Clever Gretchen* play; 1930s; $125-175. (William Biskie Collection)

Mister Archibald: *Clever Gretchen* play; 1930s; $125-175. (William Biskie Collection)

Gretel: *Hansel & Gretel* play; 1930s; $125-175. (William Biskie Collection)

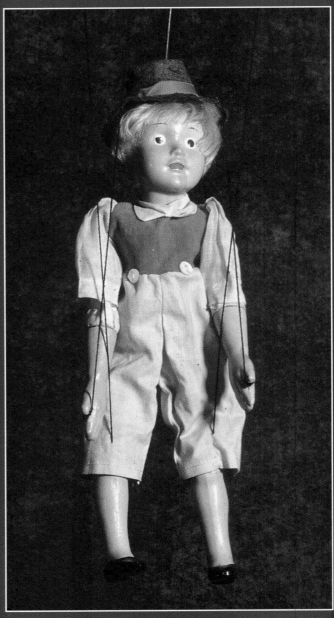

Hansel: *Hansel & Gretel* play; 1930s; $125-175. (William Biskie Collection)

142

Tippytoes, the Butler: *Lucy Lavender* play; If this is not Tippytoes, this may be Lawrence Lightfoot; 1930s; $125-175. (William Biskie Collection)

Witch: *Hansel & Gretel* play; 1930s; $125-175. (William Biskie Collection)

Lucy: *Lucy Lavender* play; 1930s; $125-175. (William Biskie Collection)

Lucy: *Lucy Lavender* play; 1930s; $125-175. (William Biskie Collection)

Pluto: Copyright Disney; Disney characters; 1930s; $200-250.
(William Biskie Collection)

Gnome: *The Enchanted Prince* play; Note the long arms; 1930s; $125-175. (William Biskie Collection)

Princess: *The Enchanted Prince* play; 1930s; $125-175. (William Biskie Collection)

Prince: *The Enchanted Prince* play; 1930s; $125-175. (William Biskie Collection)

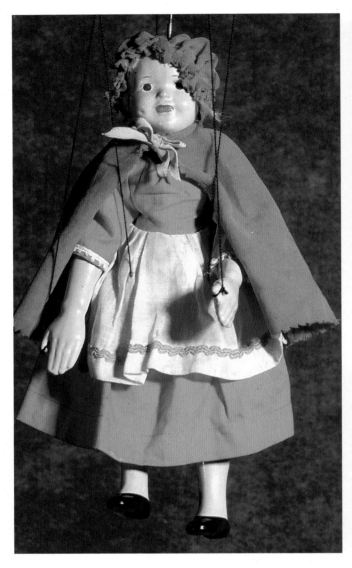

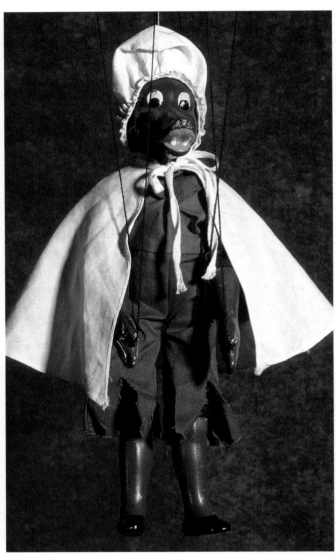

Red Riding Hood: *Little Red Riding Hood* play; 1930s; $125-175. (William Biskie Collection)

Wolf: *Little Red Riding Hood* play; 1930s; $125-175. (William Biskie Collection)

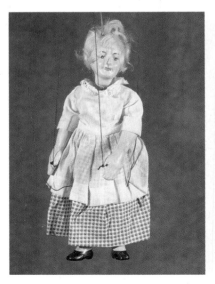

Unknown: 1930s; $75-125. (Author's Collection)

Cyrus: *Tingling Circus #2* play; 1930s; $125-175. (William Biskie Collection)

WALT DISNEY'S
MARIONETTE PLAYS

by
MADAME ALEXANDER
NEW YORK

Tony Sarg Marionette Book Cover.
(William Biskie Collection)

Donald Duck: Copyright Disney;
Wood body, movable mouth (bill);
1930s; $250-350. (Carmen & Gary
Busk Collection)

ENCORE!
storybook characters

The Brothers Grimm and Mother Goose would be impressed with the number of marionette characters inspired by folktales, children's stories, poems, and rhymes. A Red Riding Hood character was made by Tony Sarg/Madame Alexander, Hazelle's, and Pelham Puppets. Pelham made both a blonde and a brunette-haired Red Riding Hood character. Helen Haiman Joseph made a Red Riding Hood box set, including Red, Grandmother, Woodsman, and of course, the Wolf. Kings, queens, dwarfs, princes, and witches are but a few of the different storybook characters that have been made.

Shackman Company

The Shackman Company was another novelties company that included marionettes in their product line. Established in 1899 by Bertha Shackman in New York City, the Shackman Company sold a variety of products ranging from confectionery treats to imported holiday and toy novelties.

During the 1950s, Shackman's introduced their line of marionette characters. Marketed as "The Living Puppet," these marionettes are of a similar design as the British-made Pelham Puppets. Shackman's marionettes are smaller than Pelham's, measuring some 8 to 10 inches in height. Made in Japan, these puppets are of wood and cloth construction. Controls for "The Living Puppets" are a simple wood T design.

Among the different marionette characters sold by the Shackman Company are a soldier, a band leader (with a conductor's baton in hand), a clown, and Santa Claus. Shackman's marionettes are labeled with the oval gold colored "Shackman—made in Japan" paper label.

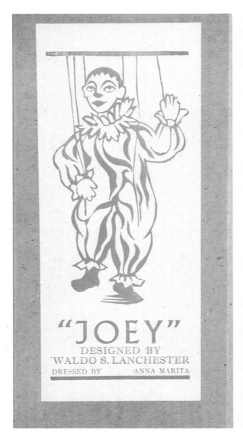

Joey Box Cover. (Carmen & Gary Busk Collection)

Joey: Waldo S. Lanchester; approximately 12 inches tall; China head, hand and feet. (Carmen & Gary Busk Collection)

Santa Claus Box
Cover. (Carmen & Gary
Busk Collection)

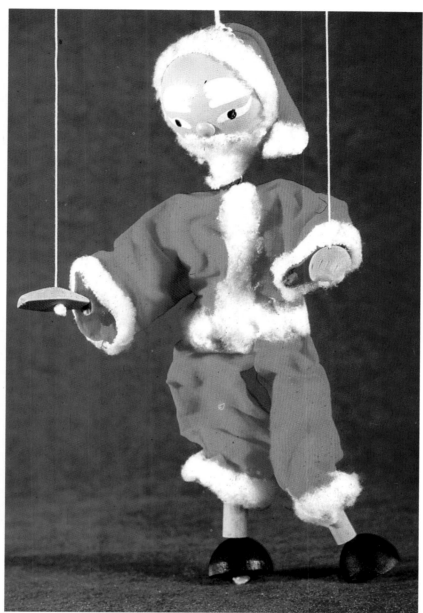

Santa Claus: Shackman,
approximately 9
inches tall; 1950s; $40-
60. (Carmen & Gary
Busk Collection)

Various Origins

The following section is an eclectic grouping of marionettes and string puppets. The lack of verifiable information in identifying a puppet's origin or its maker was the determining factor for placing a marionette in this section.

Marionettes made in Burma, Czechoslovakia, England, Sweden, and the United States are pictured herein. Characters vary from a paper-mache girl to a rubber dog, and from a composition boy scout to a porcelain clown.

Czech Marionette Stage: Hardboard and wood; multiple scenes; 1970s; $50-80 box set. (Carmen & Gary Busk Collection)

Czech Storybook King: Composition head, hands, and feet; 1970; $15-25. (Carmen & Gary Busk Collection)

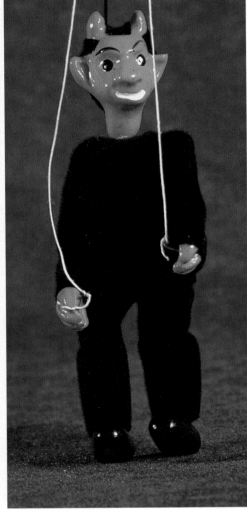

Czech Storybook Devil: Composition head, hands, and feet; 1970; $15-25. (Carmen & Gary Busk Collection)

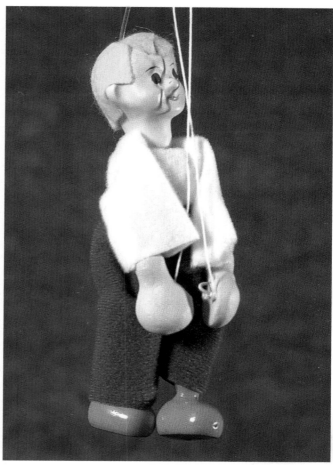

Czech Storybook Boy: Composition head, hands, and feet; 1970; $15-25. (Carmen & Gary Busk Collection)

Czech Storybook Goblin: Composition head, hands, and feet; 1970; $15-25. (Carmen & Gary Busk Collection)

Czech Marionette Box Cover: Marked "JAS"; Box contains 25 story-book characters; 1970; $15-25. (Carmen & Gary Busk Collection)

Swedish Marionette: Paper-mache head and hands; 1970s; $60-80. (Carmen & Gary Busk Collection)

Swedish Marionette: Paper-mache head and hands; 1970s; $60-80. (Carmen & Gary Busk Collection)

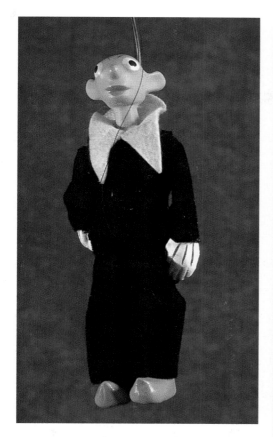

Czech Marionette: Box marked "Spejbl a Hur-vinek"; 1969; $30-50. (Carmen & Gary Busk Collection)

Czech Marionette: Box marked "Spejbl a Hur-vinek"; 1969; $30-50. (Carmen & Gary Busk Collection)

Swedish Marionette: Paper-mache head and hands; 1970s; $60-80. (Carmen & Gary Busk Collection)

Horse: Wood; Marked "Burma"; $20-40.
(Author's Collection)

Swedish Marionette: Paper-mache head and hands; 1970s; $60-80.
(Carmen & Gary Busk Collection)

Swedish Marionette: Paper-mache head and hands; 1970s; $60-80.
(Carmen & Gary Busk Collection)

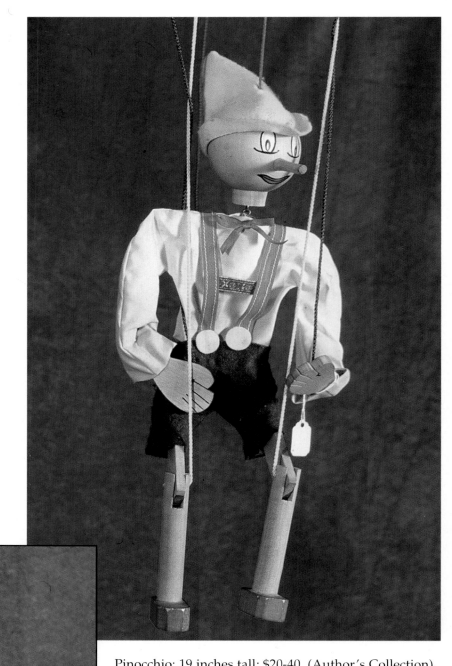

Pinocchio: 19 inches tall; $20-40. (Author's Collection)

Dog: Rubber body, felt ears; Control is rubber and shaped like a dog bone with squeeker; There is a companion character for the dog, a rubber cat with a fish-shaped control; 1960s; $40-60. (Carmen & Gary Busk Collection)

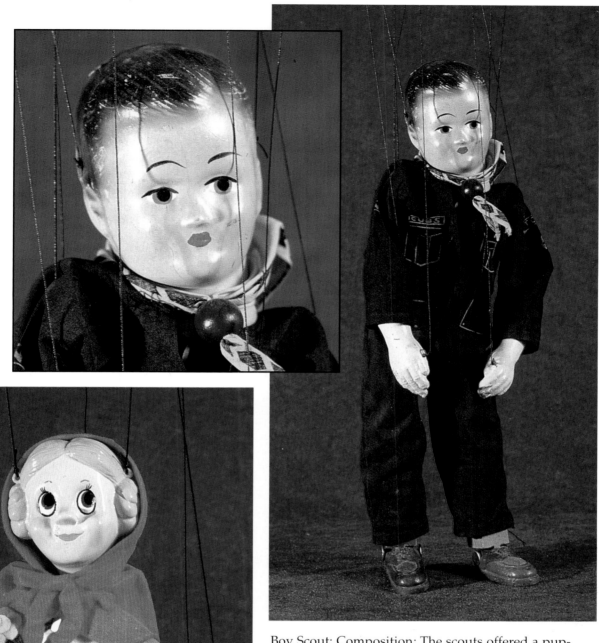

Boy Scout: Composition; The scouts offered a puppetry badge in the past for completion of assembly of this puppet kit; Note unique ankle joint; 1950s; $75-125. (Carmen & Gary Busk Collection)

Red Riding Hood: Parade Street; Construction identical to Bob Baker design; 1990s; $40-60. (Carmen & Gary Busk Collection)

Appendix

ORGANIZATION:

The Puppeteers of America, Inc.
Gayle G. Schluter
Membership Office
#5 Cricklewood Path
Pasadena, CA 91107-0102

RETAIL OUTLET:

The Puppetry Store
1525 24th St. SE
Auburn, WA 98002-7837

MUSEUM:

MacNider Museum
Mason City, Iowa
515/421-3666

The MacNider Museum houses what may be the largest Collection of Bill Baird puppets, including the famous marionettes used in the movie classic, *The Sound of Music.*

ONLINE WEB SITES:

THE PUPPETRY HOME PAGE
http://www.sagecraft.com/puppetry/

This site may be the most comprehensive puppetry related site on the Internet. It contains information on over 40 puppetry guilds distributed through eight regions across the United States, including information on the Puppeteers of America. It has information on nearly all forms of puppetry.

America Online Puppetry Folder:
The Exchange folder, Arts & Entertainment
section, Interests & Hobbies section, Puppetry folder
Host is Freshwater, freshwater@aol.com

A Maine Collectible Connection
http://www.tias.com/stores/amaine/dol-1.html

Collectors Classifieds
http://www.collectors.com/classifieds/index.html

Funk & Junk
http://www.funkandjunk.com/

Where the TOYS Are!
http://www.computrends.com/wherethetoysare/

Supermarionation
http://superm.bart.nl/puppets.html

Browse & Buy
Antiques and Collectables
http://www.antiques-colects-b-b.com/order.html

Disneyananet
http://www.disneyananet.com/dother.htm

Collectors Supermall Online
http://www.csmonline.com/

Paper Doll Bulletin Board
http://www.wwvisions.com/craftbb/paperdoll.html

rec.arts.puppetry
news:rec.arts.puppetry

TIAS - The Internet Antiques Shops
http://www.tias.com/

A Site on Collecting Marionettes
http://www.geocities.com/RodeoDrive/7266

Rare Disney Marionettes
http://vividvision.com/Marionettes.html

hjttp://collectoronline.com/booths/booth-76/

http://antiquetoy.com/class1.htm

http://collectoronline.com/booths/booth-76/

AUCTION HOUSES WITH WEB SITES
Kenneth S. Hays & Associates, Inc.
http://www.ntr.net/~auctionctr/

Billy Long Auctioneers Inc.
http://www.ntr.net/~auctionctr/

Bonhams
http://www.bonhams.com/auct/

Clints & Lam Auctions
http://www.clintsauction.com/

ONLINE AUCTION SITES

U-Auction-It
http://www.uauction.com/

ebay
http://cayman.ebay.com/aw/index.html

Bibliography

Anderton, Johana Gast. *More Twentieth Century Dolls*, Des Moines Iowa, Wallace-Homestead Book Co., 1979.

Anderton, Johana Gast. *More Twentieth Century Dolls From Bisque to Vinyl, Volume A-H*, Des Moines, Iowa, Wallace-Homestead Book Co. 1974, 1979.

Anderton, Johana Gast. *More Twentieth Century Dolls From Bisque to Vinyl, Volume I-Z*, Des Moines, Iowa, Wallace-Homestead Book Co. 1974, 1979.

Anderton, Johana Gast. *Twentieth Century Dolls From Bisque to Vinyl*, Revised Edition, North Kansas City, MO, Athena Publishing Co., 1981.

Axe, John. *Encyclopedia of Celebrity Dolls*, Cumberland Md: Hobby House Press, 1983.

Brooks, Tim and Earle Marsh. *The Complete Directory to Prime Time Network TV Shows 1946-Present*, Fifth Edition, New York, Ballantine Books, 1992.

Busby, Marjean. "Puppets Populated Her Life," *The Kansas City Star Magazine*, June 16, 1993.

Davis, Stephen. *Say Kids! What Time Is It?: Notes From the Peanut Gallery*, Boston, Little, Brown, and Co., 1987.

Flynn, Jane Fifield. Kansas City Women of Independent Minds.

Hunt, Tamara Robin. *Tony Sarg: Puppeteer In America, 1915-42*, North Vancouver, Canada, Charlemagne Press, 1988.

Lapham, Jim. "Puppet Maker," *The Kansas City Star Magazine*, May 23, 1973.

Leech, David. *Yours Puppetually*, Issue No. 1 (Spring 1996), Issue No. 2 (Summer 1996), Issue No. 3 (Autumn 1996), Issue No. 4 (Winter 1996/97), Issue No. 5 (Spring 1997), Issue No. 6 & 7 (Autumn 1997), David Leech Productions, Weymouth, Dorset, Great Britain.

McPharlin, Paul. *Puppets in America: 1739 to Today, with an account of the first American Puppetry Conference*, Detroit, Michigan, 1936.

Mobley, Jane "A Razzle-Dazzle of Puppets Bids Farewell," *Star*, September 23, 1979.

Revi, Albert Christian. *Spinning Wheels Complete Book of Dolls*, New York, Galahad Books, 1975.

Smith, Patricia R. *Modern Collectors Dolls* Third Series, Paducah, KY: Collector Books, New York; dist. by Crown Publishers, 1976.

Smith, Patricia R. *Modern Collectors Dolls*, Second Series, New York; Crown Publishers, 1975.

Smith, Patricia R. *Modern Collectors Dolls*, First Edition, Paducah KY, Collector Books, 1973.

Von Boehn, Max. *Puppets & Automata*, New York, NY, Dover Publications, 1972.

Index

About the author

Daniel E. Hodges has been an avid collector for more than 25 years, and has been a frequent attendee of antique auctions for more than 15 years. His first serious collection—beer cans—was started while he was in junior high school. Daniel and his wife, Melinda, have other active collections as well, including Haviland china, dolls, pickle castors, miniatures, antique furniture, and antique lighting fixtures, which he refurbishes and restores.

The love of antiques and collecting fits right in, and even helps, to furnish and decorate the three Victorian houses Daniel and his wife are renovating in the historic Sherman Hill neighborhood, located in Des Moines, Iowa.

It was during an auction foray several years back that Daniel's wife purchased three marionettes, Hazelle's Sailor, Penny and a Burmese horse. The lack of information piqued his curiosity, which led him to research the history of the unique stringed puppets called marionettes. This is his first book.